AF450145

MAYA A

BREAKING THE SILENCE

Illuminating the intricacies of borderline personality disorder and its profound influence on relationships

Contents

Foreword — iii

Preface — viii

1 Introduction — 1

2 Structure of The Book Subject wise — 4

3 What is DSM-5 and Explaining Borderline Personality Disorder — 7

4 Advance Studies By Various Institutions in Helping Better... — 17

5 The Development and Causes of Borderline Personality... — 26

6 The Symptoms and Subtype of Borderline Personality... — 47

7 Difficulty In Relationship; Understanding Borderline... — 52

8 Fear Of Abandonment- A HALLMARK SYMPTOM of Borderline... — 55

9 Borderline Personality Disorder and it's Impact on Various... — 64

10 Preparing for Treatment: Gearing Yourself and Family and... — 67

11 "Handling Emergency Situations: Calling 911" — 73

12 Treatment Options for Borderline Personality Disorder ... — 78

13	Living with BPD: Self-Care, Self-help and Coping Strategies	81
14	Few Critical Issues of Young Adults Borderline Personality...	85
15	Case Studies of Few BPD Persons in Different Situations	93
16	Handling BPD with the help of Dialectical Behavior Therapy...	116
17	Checklist for BPD Persons: 10 Steps for Successful & Happy...	127
18	YOGA; 5 Yoga Exercises for Overall Well-being	132
19	Mindfulness Techniques for Self Help	137
20	Some Suggestion For Treatment And Research Advancements...	142
21	Websites(Suggested) For More Learning Information on...	144
22	Knowing and Building Your Support Network	147
23	Conclusion	151
24	Inspire Someone Else!	154
25	Resources	156
	About the Author	158
	Also by Maya A	160

Foreword

A few Important Reviews About the Book ;

Review by a psychotherapist for over 30 years treating borderline personality disorder.

5.0 out of 5 stars. **A MUST READ !!!**
  Reviewed in the United States on April 21, 2024

As a psychotherapist for over 30 years treating borderline personality disorder, I found this book to be an absolute must-read. It takes a deep dive into precisely what BPD is and the symptoms and impact. It also covers treatment options and self-care for people with BPD. The biggest issue with BPD is the total fear of being abandoned, and this book does a great job of explaining that. BPD is very disruptive to the person with BPD and to the people that love them. This offers guidance and hope. **I HIGHLY RECOMMEND!!**

****

5.0 out of 5 stars **Great Information!**
  Reviewed in the United States on May 7, 2024

****

Really interesting!
 Reviewed in the United Kingdom on January 17, 2024
 Verified Purchase

This is an incredibly interesting, informative, well-researched, well-presented, and engaging read! While on the shorter side, it's packed with fascinating information, and is well worth the relatively cheap price which it's currently being sold at. I highly recommend giving this a go if you're interested as it isn't a huge commitment to read, and is sure to teach you something new. 5/5!

****

super insightful...5 stars
 Reviewed in the United States on March 12, 2024
 Verified Purchase

"Breaking the Silence" is super insightful for anyone seeking to better understand Borderline Personality Disorder (BPD) and how it impacts the person's everyday life and relationships.

I would have to say that this information is especially critical and helpful for anyone who works in the education system. It gives some real tools you can actually teach or use with your students affected by BPD to help manage their emotions and get along better with peers and ensure a positive learning environment for everyone.

This book is well-organized and provides you with all the key info about BPD in a way that's easy to swallow. It's like a crash course in understanding and dealing with BPD.

Bottom line?, "Breaking the Silence" is a must-read for anyone seeking a better understanding of BPD and its impact on personal and interpersonal dynamics. I'm giving it five stars and highly recommend it to anyone seeking insight into this complex disorder.

****

6 Star book

Reviewed in the United States on April 1, 2024

I would give this book a 6th star if I could. As I was reading it, I was thinking back to someone I knew from my past, who fit the description of someone with a personality disorder.

This is something that is not often discussed, but so very important, and the author did a beautiful job of educating the reader. Bravo!

****

5.0 out of 5 stars **Best Book to learn about Borderline Personality Disorder!**

Reviewed in the United States on February 6, 2024

So, I am aware of mental health issues and the types of mental health issues that some people go through. But I was never that well informed about borderline personality disorder (BPD) and "Breaking the Silence" is a great book that explores borderline personality disorder and how it affects the lives of people who have it.

"Breaking the Silence" is a book that helps readers learn more about borderline personality disorder (BPD) and how to deal with this disorder in a healthy way, as well as learning how to manage your emotions and improving your relationships with your families and friends.

Maya A. did a fantastic job at writing this book as this book does a fantastic job at explaining to the audience about what borderline personality disorder (BPD) is and how to deal with this disorder. The fact that having borderline personality disorder can sometimes affect your relationships with your family and friends due to being afraid of abandonment and being impulsive in your decisions, has really made me open my eyes to this disorder and I like the fact that this book helps explain to readers about how to handle borderline personality disorder in a healthy way that can help repair your relationships with your friends and family.

Overall, "Breaking the Silence" is a fantastic book that teaches people about borderline personality disorder (BPD) and how to deal with this disorder in a positive way. I would highly recommend this book to anyone who wants to learn more about borderline personality disorder.

Preface

Anything human is mentionable, and anything mentionable can be more manageable. When we can talk about our feelings, they become less overwhelming, less upsetting, and less scary." — Fred Rogers.

Do you often see people around you behaving very strangely by reacting to smallest issues too strongly and surprises you as "what the hell " & why is he/she behaving in this way" and you fail to understand reason behind such a behavior ?

Have you ever felt like you're on an emotional roller coaster? Do intense emotions rule your life?

Do you or someone you love face any of the following:

- Always quiet and often feeling emptiness in your life?
- Relationships feeling like roller coasters?
- Are office relationships full of turmoil?
- Feelings of impulsiveness or low self-esteem?
- You may experience dramatic mood shifts, from feeling incredibly happy to utterly empty. Perhaps your relationships feel unstable, with constant highs and lows.

If this sounds familiar, you might be wondering if Borderline Personality Disorder (BPD) could be a factor.

This book can help you understand BPD in an easier way and suggest you to learn as how to manage it.

Whether seeking answers for yourself or a loved one, this book comprehensively explores this complex issue in straightforward language and provides clear and practical guidance on BPD.

Here's what you'll discover inside:

- **Knowing and understanding BPD from the perspective of various well known organizations** ; Gain a clear picture of the disorder and how it might impact your life.
- **Knowing and understanding various aspects of BPD like, symptoms of emotional instability, disturbed self images ,impulsivity**; Gain a clear knowledge as to how these are adversely affecting your life and life of people around you .
- **Learning to Take Control of Your Emotions:** Learn practical tools and strategies for managing intense feelings and building emotional resilience.
- **Knowing How to Build Healthy Relationships:** Discover how to foster more nutritious and stable connections with the people you care about.
- **Finding hope and supporting case of your need:** This book is a beacon of hope, offering a path towards a brighter future and a supportive community of understanding.

- **Finding ways to manage these well by various methods**; details are given in succeeding chapters.
- **I offer practical tools and coping mechanisms, including yoga techniques, mindfulness exercises, and additional resources that readers can readily apply to their lives**

In "Breaking the Silence," considering the substantial stigma surrounding BPD people in the society, seeking treatment or help can also be quite challenging for individuals with this disorder. Therefore, I emphasize providing relevant and necessary knowledge to help readers identify challenging patterns, recognize symptoms, and foster self-acceptance through self-compassion despite the disorder's associated difficulties.

1

Introduction

Mental health problems don't define who you are. They are something you experience. You walk in the rain, and you feel the rain, but, importantly, YOU ARE NOT THE RAIN." — Matt Haig.

BPD (Borderline Personality Disorder) is a multifaceted mental health condition characterized by a pattern of unstable emotions, self-image, and relationships impacting emotional regulation, self-perception, and interpersonal relationships. It affects approximately 1-2% of the population, and while women are diagnosed slightly more often, men can also experience BPD. I attempt to bring out this issue in a way that people from all walks of life can understand well.

Borderline Personality Disorder is a common condition that is thought to occur globally, with a prevalence of 0.2-1.8% in the general population. Higher prevalence rates are found in clinical populations. Moran et al. found a prevalence rate of 4-6% among primary care attendees, suggesting that people with BPD are more likely to visit their general practitioner. Chanen et al. reported a prevalence rate of 11% in adolescent outpatients and 49% in adolescent inpatients. The highest prevalence has been found in people requiring the most intensive level of care, with a rate of 60-80% among patients in forensic services.

Borderline Personality Disorder also has a significant impact on relationships. The intense emotional reactions and fear of abandonment can create a turbulent dynamic in romantic partnerships. Individuals with BPD may struggle with trust, have difficulty maintaining boundaries, and exhibit patterns of idealization and devaluation towards their partners. These patterns can strain relationships and lead to frequent conflicts and emotional volatility.

Family relationships can also be affected by BPD. The intense emotions and unstable sense of self can impact parent-child relationships and sibling dynamics. Family members may have to struggle to understand and support their loved ones with BPD, leading to strained communication and emotional tension.

Friendships can be challenging for individuals with BPD as well. The fear of rejection and shifting self-image can make maintaining stable and fulfilling friendships difficult. The intense emotions experienced by individuals with BPD can also be overwhelming for friends, leading to strained relationships if not adequately understood and managed.

The high prevalence and increased suicide rate in patients with BPD make an unassailable argument that effective treatment needs to be developed and that treatment has to be widely available. While some treatments for BPD are moderately effective in randomized controlled trials, it remains of considerable concern that most of them require extensive training, making them unavailable to most patients.

It is essential to note that with the proper treatment and support, individuals with BPD can learn to manage their symptoms and cultivate healthier relationships. Therapies such as Dialectical Behavior Therapy (DBT) are known to be effective in helping individuals with BPD regulate their emotions, improve interpersonal skills, and develop coping strategies.

But you don't have to go through this alone!

BPD can increase the risk of depression, anxiety, substance abuse, and self-harm. However, with the proper treatment and support, you can manage these symptoms and live a fulfilling life. This book will explore practical ways to help you regulate emotions, develop healthy coping mechanisms, and build stronger relationships.

2

Structure of The Book Subject wise

The structure of this book is as follows:

Chapters 2 to 5:

- We are providing readers with an understanding of Border-line Personality Disorders (BPDs), learning about DSM-5, Advancement in understanding .

Chapters 6 to 8:

- Here, I will be talking about the root causes of Borderline Personality Disorder, its Symptoms & various subtypes, and the impact of multiple factors of BPD on relationships, difficulty in relationships, and above all, the fear of abandonment in relationships.

Chapters 9 to 11:

- Borderline Personality Disorder and its Impact on Various

Relationships, Preparing for Treatment: Gearing Yourself and Family and Friends Up To Move Forward, and "Handling Emergency Situations: Calling 911".

Chapter 12:

- Discussing Various Treatment Options for Borderline Personality Disorder People.

Chapters 13 to 14:

- I am discussing aspects of living with Borderline Personality Disorder persons & Challenges, and also examining critical situations among teens, and focusing on suicide risk.

Chapter 15:
I present a few case studies to illustrate how individuals manage their BPD issues to improve their lives.

Chapter 16:
Here I briefly discuss Dialectical Behavior Therapy (DBT) techniques for managing Borderline Personality Disorder.

Chapter 17:

- Checklist for BPD Person: This checklist includes ten simple steps to ease the effects of BPD and promote a happier life.

Chapters 18 to 19:

I will introduce practical strategies, such as beneficial yoga, mindfulness techniques, and exercises for individuals with borderline personality disorder. Incorporation will immensely help people with BPD to live a better life.

Chapters 20 to 23:

I am talking about advanced treatment options for BPD cases. Some Suggestions For Treatment And Research Advancements Association For Personality Disorder and providing knowledge information on additional resources for building support network.

3

What is DSM-5 and Explaining Borderline Personality Disorder

Now I aim to familiarize my readers with the standard guide-lines for diagnosing Borderline Personality Disorder.

Understanding DSM-5;

The **DSM-5, short for the Diagnostic and Statistical Manual of Mental Disorders, Fifth Edition,** is a widely used manual published by the American Psychiatric Association. It provides a standardized criteria and classification system for diagnosing mental disorders.

According to the DSM-5, Borderline Personality Disorder

(BPD) is characterized by a pervasive pattern of instability in interpersonal relationships, self-image, and emotions.

Structure of the DSM-5

The DSM-5 is organized into sections, each focusing on a specific category of mental disorders. Here are some relevant sections for our discussion:

- **Section I: Diagnostic Criteria and Other Coding Systems:** This section contains the core diagnostic criteria for all mental disorders listed in the DSM-5, including BPD.
- **Section II: Text Revision (TR):** This section provides additional information on specific disorders, including prevalence rates, risk factors, differential diagnoses, and treatment approaches. While not a standalone document, the Text Revision (TR) is often referenced alongside the core diagnostic criteria.
- **Section III: Emerging Measures and Models:** This section contains proposed criteria for disorders not formally included in the DSM-5 but warrants further research.

Diagnosing Mental Disorders with the DSM-5

The DSM-5 utilizes a multi-axial system for diagnosing mental disorders. While this system is no longer the primary method in the latest revision (DSM-5-TR), it's helpful to understand its historical context:

- **Axis I:** Clinically Significant Disorders and Other Conditions That May Be a Focus of Clinical Attention – This axis encompasses the core mental disorders, including BPD.
- **Axis II:** Personality Disorders and Intellectual Disabilities – This axis focuses on personality disorders like BPD. (No longer used in DAM-5-TR)
- **Axis III:** General Medical Conditions – This axis documented any co-occurring medical conditions.
- **Axis IV:** Psycho-social and Environmental Problems—This axis captured relevant social and environmental factors contributing to mental disorders.
- **Axis V:** Assessment of Global Functioning (AGF) – This axis provided a score reflecting an individual's overall functioning in various life domains. (No longer used in DSM-5-TR)

The current DSM-5 emphasizes a dimensional approach, focusing on the severity of symptoms rather than a definite diagnosis on some axes.

Borderline Personality Disorder (BPD) in the DSM-5

BPD falls under the category of Personality Disorders in the DSM-5. Personality disorders are characterized by inflexible and maladaptive patterns of thinking, feeling, behaving, and relating to others that significantly deviate from cultural expectations and cause distress or impairment in functioning.

Diagnosing BPD: The Criteria

The DSM-5 outlines specific criteria that a person must meet to receive a diagnosis of BPD. An individual needs to experience at least five of the following nine criteria for at least one year, causing significant impairment in their life:

1. **Frantic efforts to avoid real or imagined abandonment.** This intense fear of being alone can lead to desperate clinginess or manipulation to keep relationships intact.
2. **A pattern of unstable and intense interpersonal relationships characterized by alternating between extremes of idealization and devaluation.** People with BPD may idealize new partners, seeing them as perfect, but then quickly switch to anger and devaluation when perceived flaws emerge (splitting).
3. **Identity disturbance is a markedly and persistently unstable self-image or sense of self. It can manifest as difficulty in consistently understanding one's identity, values, or** goals.
4. **Impulsivity in at least two areas that are potentially self-damaging, for example, spending, substance abuse, reckless driving, sex, and binge eating.** Impulsive behaviors can be a way to cope with intense emotions or a fleeting sense of control.
5. **Recurrent suicidal behavior, gestures, threats, or self-harming behavior.** These acts can be a cry for help, a response to overwhelming emotions, or a way to manage pain.
6. **Chronic feelings of emptiness.** A pervasive sense of lack of purpose or meaning can be a significant struggle for people with BPD.

7. **Inappropriate, intense anger or difficulty controlling anger (e.g., frequent displays of temper, constant anger, recurrent physical fights).** Difficulties managing anger can damage relationships and lead to impulsive actions.

8. **Transient, stress-related episodes of dissociation or derealization.** Dissociation involves feeling disconnected from oneself or one's surroundings, while derealization is experiencing the environment as unreal.

9. **Significant impairment in functioning in one or more areas, such as social, work, or school.** The symptoms of BPD can significantly impact a person's ability to maintain healthy relationships, hold a job, or perform well in school.

To confirm that a person suffers from BPD and person has needs to receive a diagnosis, one exhibiting at least five of these criteria. It's important to note that a qualified mental health professional must make a diagnosis based on a comprehensive assessment of symptoms and history. The DSM-5 criteria provide a framework for understanding and diagnosing BPD, and they should not be used as a self-diagnostic tool.

The DSM-5: A Standard Reference;

The DSM-5, published by the American Psychiatric Association (APA), is the authoritative guide used by mental health professionals in the USA to diagnose mental disorders. It provides clinicians with a common language and criteria for consistent and reliable diagnoses.

The DSM-5 categorizes mental disorders into various categories based on shared characteristics. **Borderline Personality Disorder falls under Cluster B and is characterized by dramatic, erratic, and emotional behaviors.**

Beyond the Criteria: Understanding the Spectrum;

It's important to remember that BPD exists on a spectrum. People may experience some, but not all, of the criteria, and symptoms' severity can vary greatly. The DSM-5 provides a framework for diagnosis, but a good clinician will take a comprehensive history to understand the individual's unique presentation.

Limitations of the DSM-5;

While the DSM-5 is a valuable tool, it has limitations.

- **Focus on Symptoms, not Causes:** The DSM-5 doesn't delve into the underlying causes of BPD, which can be complex and involve a combination of genetic, environmental, and developmental factors.
- **Categorical System vs. Dimensional Approach:** The DSM-5 uses a definite system, meaning someone either meets the criteria for a disorder or doesn't. However, some argue a dimensional approach would be more accurate, reflecting the varying degrees of symptom severity.
- **Stigma:** The labels associated with mental disorders can carry stigma, and BPD is no exception. Focusing on the individual's experience rather than just the diagnosis is

essential.

Beyond Diagnosis: Treatment Options;

A diagnosis of BPD from the DSM-5 is just the first step. Fortunately, various evidence-based therapies can effectively manage BPD symptoms and improve quality of life. Some commonly used approaches include:

- **Dialectical Behavior Therapy (DBT):** This skills-based therapy teaches emotional regulation, mindfulness, distress tolerance, and interpersonal effectiveness.
- **Cognitive behavioral therapy (CBT) helps individuals identify and change negative thought patterns that contribute** to their emotions and behaviors.
- **Mentalization-Based Therapy (MBT):** This therapy focuses on understanding one's and others' mental states to improve communication and relationships.

The Power (and Limitations) of Criteria;

The DSM-5 offers a standardized set of diagnostic criteria for BPD. If met to a specific degree, these criteria guide clinicians in diagnosing the disorder. However, viewing these criteria as a compass, not a rigid map, is essential.

- **Core Features, Varied Expressions:** The nine core criteria in the DSM-5 capture the essence of BPD: fear of abandonment, unstable relationships, identity disturbance, impulsivity, self-harm, chronic emptiness, anger problems, dissociation, and functional impairment. However, how these features manifest can differ significantly from person to person; someone with BPD might experience an intense fear of abandonment but struggle less with self-harm, while another might exhibit frequent self-harming behaviors but manage more stable relationships.

- **Severity Spectrum:** The spectrum concept is fundamental in understanding BPD. The severity of each criterion can fluctuate over time and vary across individuals. Some may exhibit mild, occasional episodes of dissociation compared to others who experience frequent and debilitating dissociative episodes. Recognizing this spectrum helps tailor treatment approaches to individual needs.
- **Comorbidity and Overlap:** BPD often co-occurs with other mental health conditions like depression, anxiety, or substance abuse. This can further complicate the presentation and make the diagnosis more nuanced. Symptoms of BPD might overlap with other disorders, requiring a careful clinical evaluation to differentiate them.

Looking Beyond the Checkbox:

While the DSM-5 offers valuable criteria, it doesn't encompass the complete picture of BPD. Here's where understanding the spectrum becomes crucial:

- **Individualized Experiences:** The DSM-5 criteria provide a starting point, but a thorough clinical assessment must delve into the individual's personal history, trauma experiences, and unique presentation. Understanding the "why" behind the symptoms unlocks more effective treatment options.

- **Developmental Context:** The onset and presentation of BPD can vary depending on a person's developmental stage. Childhood experiences like neglect, abuse, or unstable environments can contribute to the development of BPD traits. Recognizing these developmental contexts provides a deeper understanding of the individual's struggles.
- **Cultural Considerations:** Cultural background can influence people's emotions and behaviors. The DSM-5 criteria may not always translate perfectly across diverse cultures. Culturally sensitive assessment is crucial to avoid misdiagnosis.

Moving Beyond Labels: The Importance of Functioning;

The true impact of Borderline Personality Disorder lies in its functional impairment. The DSM-5 emphasizes how these criteria translate into difficulties maintaining relationships, holding a job, or managing daily activities. The severity of this functional impairment becomes a critical factor in diagnosis and treatment planning.

- **Levels of Functioning:** The DSM-5 doesn't categorize BPD into subtypes based on severity. However, some clinicians use the Global Assessment of Functioning (GAF) scale to assess overall functioning in various life domains. This can provide a more nuanced understanding of how BPD impacts the individual.
- **Resilience and Strengths:** The spectrum of BPD also en-

compasses resilience and strengths. Some individuals with BPD display remarkable coping abilities, vital creativity, and intense emotional depth. Highlighting these strengths can be crucial in the recovery process.

Hence, DSM-5 is A Spectrum of Experiences, Not a Monolith

The DSM-5 serves as a valuable tool for diagnosing BPD and ensuring consistent diagnoses. However, understanding BPD solely through the lens of criteria misses the intricate spectrum of experiences individuals grapple with. Recognizing the variability in symptom presentation, severity, and individual context allows for a more comprehensive appreciation of BPD and opens doors for personalized treatment plans.

It's important to note that:

- *The DSM-5 criteria are not a checklist; a mental health professional must conduct a comprehensive evaluation to diagnose BPD.*
- *The severity of symptoms can vary significantly among individuals diagnosed with BPD.*
- *The DSM-5 emphasizes.*

4

Advance Studies By Various Institutions in Helping Better Understanding Of Borderline Personality Disorder

Several critical studies conducted by various institutions, including the Mayo Clinic, the National Institute of Mental Health (NIGH), the American Psychological Association (APA), and Johns Hopkins University, have significantly enhanced our understanding of Borderline Personality Disorder (BPD).

While DSM-5 serves as a valuable tool and benchmark for diagnosing BPD and ensuring consistent diagnoses, understanding BPD solely through the lens of criteria misses the intricate spectrum of experiences individuals grapple with. There are several prominent institutions whose significant contributions have significantly advanced our understanding of borderline personality disorder. Reading these will help in better understanding of Borderline Personality Disorder. Among the numerous studies on BPD, some particularly notable ones are conducted by the following institutions:

- **Mayo Clinic:** Mayo Clinic, a world-renowned non-profit medical center based in the USA, provides a wealth of information on Borderline Personality Disorder (BPD).
- **National Institute of Mental Health (NIMH):** The National Institute of Mental Health offers in-depth information on BPD, including research updates, causes, symptoms, diagnosis, treatments, and resources for people with BPD and their loved ones (https://www.nimh.nih.gov /health/ topics/borderline-personality-disorder), is instrumental.
- **American Psychological Association (APA):** The American Psychological Association website offers resources on BPD, including information on diagnosis, treatment options, and coping strategies (https://dictionary.apa.org/borderline-personality-disorder).
- **John Hopkins University** in understanding and its role in Borderline Personality Disorder.

Studies by the Mayo Clinic and its contribution to Borderline Personality Disorder (BPD)

The Mayo Clinic, a world-renowned non-profit medical center based in the USA, provides a wealth of information on Borderline Personality Disorder (BPD) but doesn't have specific contributions to the diagnostic criteria outlined in the DSM-5. Mayo Clinic helps explain BPD as follows:

Leveraging the Mayo Clinic's Resources

The Mayo Clinic website offers a comprehensive and user-friendly resource for understanding Borderline personality disorder. Here are some helpful information:

- **Symptoms and Causes:** Summarize the core symptoms of BPD as outlined by the Mayo Clinic, including fear of abandonment, unstable relationships, impulsive behaviors, self-harm, emotional dysregulation, and identity disturbance. You can also discuss potential contributing factors like genetics, brain development, and environmental factors such as childhood trauma or neglect.
- **Diagnosis and Treatment:** A mental health professional diagnoses BPD using a combination of clinical interviews and psychological evaluations. The Mayo Clinic offers various treatment options, including Dialectical Behavior Therapy (DBT), Cognitive Behavioral Therapy (CBT), and medication management.
- **Living with BPD:** The Mayo Clinic also offers valuable

resources on coping with BPD and maintaining healthy relationships. These resource tips can be incorporated into our lifestyle to manage emotions, build healthy communication skills, and reduce self-harming behaviors. Self-care and building a solid support system are also essential parts of treatment.

The National Institute of Mental Health (NIMH) and its contribution to Borderline Personality Disorder (BPD)

The **National Institute of Mental Health (NIMH)** is also a crucial contributor to the understanding and treatment of Borderline Personality Disorder (BPD) in the USA. While the NIMH doesn't directly set diagnostic criteria like the DSM-5, their extensive research efforts play a crucial role in:

- **Funding research on BPD:** The NIMH provides grants to researchers across the country to study BPD. This research helps us understand its causes, risk factors, best treatment approaches, and potential new therapies.
- **Raising awareness about BPD:** The NIMH disseminates information about BPD to the public and mental health professionals. This includes educational materials, fact sheets, and public awareness campaigns that help reduce stigma and encourage people to seek help.

- **Developing treatment guidelines:** The NIMH develops evidence-based treatment guidelines for BPD based on research findings. These guidelines help clinicians provide the most effective care to their patients.

Following are a few meaningful & essential contributions of NIMH in understanding the BPD:

Highlighting Research Advancements:

- Funding ongoing research on BPD.
- NIMH has in its credit some key research findings, such as the connection between childhood trauma and BPD or the effectiveness of specific therapies.
- Emphasize the ongoing nature of research and the hope it brings for better understanding and treatment in the future.

Dispelling Myths and Stigma:

- NIMH's public awareness campaigns are pivotal in debunking misconceptions about BPD.
- NIMH provides accessible resources to the public, including its website and educational brochures.

Focusing on Treatment Options:

- Evidence-based treatments for BPD emphasize the role of the NIMH in developing treatment guidelines.
- They focus on dialectical behavior therapy (DBT) and cognitive behavioral therapy (CBT), highlighting their effectiveness based on research supported by the NIMH.

It's important to acknowledge the significant contributions of NIMH in demonstrating ongoing research efforts and progress in understanding and treating BPD.

The American Psychological Association (APA) and its role in Borderline Personality Disorder (BPD).

The American Psychological Association (APA) plays a crucial role in disseminating information about Borderline Personality Disorder (BPD) in the USA, though it doesn't directly set diagnostic criteria like the DSM-5.

Highlighting the APA's Contributions:

Focus on Knowledge Dissemination

- **APA Dictionary of Psychology:** The APA publishes the authoritative Dictionary of Psychology, which provides a clear and concise definition of BPD and outlines the core symptoms and diagnostic criteria.
- **APA Journals and Publications:** The APA publishes various scholarly journals and resources on mental health. Consider mentioning some relevant articles or research findings that explore BPD causes, treatment options, or the lived experience of individuals with BPD.
- **APA Public Education:** The APA website offers resources to help the public understand mental health conditions. Highlight the availability of these resources on the APA website (https://dictionary.apa.org/borderline-personality-disorder) for readers seeking more information.

Promoting Evidence-Based Practices

- **APA Practice Guidelines:** While the APA doesn't set diagnostic criteria, it promotes evidence-based treatment approaches for various mental health conditions. You can discuss how the APA emphasizes treatments like dialectical behavior therapy (DBT) and cognitive behavioral therapy (CBT) for BPD, which have proven effective through research.
- **Ethical Considerations:** The APA emphasizes ethical guidelines for psychologists. You can mention the importance of these ethical considerations in diagnosing and treating

BPD, ensuring patient well-being, and fostering respectful interactions.

The Contribution of Johns Hopkins University to Understanding Borderline Personality Disorder

Johns Hopkins University is renowned as a prestigious institution, particularly in medical research, with significant contributions towards understanding Borderline Personality Disorder (BPD). Here are some contributions that Johns Hopkins University has made toward understanding Borderline Personality Disorder (BPD):

1. **Research Studies:** Johns Hopkins researchers may have investigated various aspects of BPD, such as its etiology, treatment efficacy, and underlying neurobiology. These studies could provide valuable insights into the mechanisms of Borderline Personality Disorder and its effective management.
2. **Look at Departments and Centers:** Johns Hopkins has various departments and centers related to mental health research. Exploring their websites can reveal ongoing research projects related to BPD. Some relevant areas might be the Department of Psychiatry and Behavioral Science or the Mood Disorders Center.
3. **General Contribution:** Johns Hopkins contributes to BPD

research in various ways. This includes studies on:

- **Causes and risk factors of BPD**
- **Brain abnormalities associated with BPD**
- **Treatment options for BPD**
- **The effectiveness of specific therapies for BPD**

Exploring the avenues mentioned above should provide a comprehensive understanding of Johns Hopkins' significant contributions to enhancing our understanding of BPD.

5

The Development and Causes of Borderline Personality Disorder

"Sometimes the people around you won't understand your journey. They don't need to; it's not for them." —Joubert Botha.

Borderline Personality Disorder (BPD) is complex and multi-faceted, and its development involves a combination of genetic, environmental, and neuro-biological factors. This is not developed overnight but is the culmination of many factors. Although the exact causes are not fully understood, various factors acting as potential contributors to the development of BPD have been identified:

The Development And Causes Of Borderline Personality Disorder

1. Genetic Factors:

Research suggests that there is a genetic component to Borderline Personality Disorders. Studies have shown that individuals with a family history of BPD or other mood disorders are more likely to develop the condition themselves. However, specific genes associated with BPD have not been identified yet, and multiple genes and gene-environment interactions likely play a role.

2. Environmental Factors:

A few environmental factors creating BPD are adverse childhood experiences, such as physical or sexual abuse, neglect, or unstable family environments, which are strongly associated with the development of BPD. These experiences can disrupt normal emotional and social development, leading to difficulties in emotion regulation, self-identity, and interpersonal relationships.

3. Neurobiological Factors:

Brain imaging studies have revealed differences in the structure and function of the brain in individuals with BPD. Areas of the brain involved in emotional regulation, impulse control, and social cognition, namely the amygdala, prefrontal cortex, and anterior cingulate cortex, may be affected. Neurochemical imbalances, particularly involving serotonin and dopamine, have also been implicated in BPD.

4. Invalidating Environments:

Growing up in an invalidating environment wherein the emotions of the person having BPD are consistently ignored, dismissed, or invalidated can contribute to the development of Borderline Personality Disorder. This can result in difficulties recognizing and regulating emotions and a heightened sensitivity to rejection or abandonment.

It is essential to know that while these factors may contribute to increasing the risk of developing BPD, not everyone with these risk factors will develop this Disorder. BPD is a complex condition influenced by a combination of factors, and individual experiences and resilience also play a significant role.

Let me elaborate more on these four basic factors for better understanding of development and causes Of Borderline Personality Disorder.

Understanding the development and causes of BPD is crucial for effective treatment and support. Psychotherapies, such as Dialectical Behavior Therapy (DBT), focus on helping individuals develop skills for emotion regulation, distress tolerance, and interpersonal effectiveness. These therapies can be highly effective in managing the symptoms and improving the overall quality of life for individuals with BPD;

I-Understanding the Genetic Factors, Predisposition to Borderline Personality Disorder and Building Resilience; Navigating the Labyrinth:

Borderline Personality Disorder (BPD) is a complex condition characterized by intense emotions, unstable relationships, and a distorted self-image. While the exact cause of BPD remains elusive, research suggests a significant role for genetics. This chapter explores the potential influence of genes on BPD development and equips you with practical strategies to navigate this labyrinth and build resilience.

The Genetic Landscape of BPD

While specific genes haven't been pinpointed for BPD, research suggests a genetic predisposition might increase vulnerability. Here's how genes might influence BPD:

- **Emotional Sensitivity:** Some people may be genetically predisposed to experience emotions more intensely. When combined with environmental stressors, this heightened sensitivity can make it challenging to manage emotions effectively.
- **Stress Response System:** Genetic factors might influence the stress response system. This system may become hyperactive when faced with stressful situations, leading to difficulties coping with emotional distress.

Genes Load the Gun, But You Aim the Trigger

It's important to remember that genes aren't destiny. Environmental factors and your response to them significantly impact how your genes influence your life. Here's why this is empowering:

- **Focus on Controllable:** You can't change your genes, but you can control your reactions to situations and develop coping mechanisms to manage your emotions. This proactive approach empowers you to manage BPD symptoms.
- **Minimize Triggers:** Identify situations or behaviors that trigger intense emotions. Once you recognize these triggers, you can develop strategies to avoid or manage them effectively.
- **Prioritize Self-Care:** Taking care of your physical and mental health is crucial. Getting enough sleep, eating healthy meals, and exercising regularly promote overall

well-being and emotional regulation.

Building Resilience: Strategies for Managing Borderline Personality Disorder

While genes may play a role, you have the power to build resilience and manage BPD symptoms. Here are some practical steps you can take:

- **Therapy is Key:** A therapist specializing in Borderline Personality Disorder can provide crucial support and guidance. Therapy can equip you with skills to manage emotions, build healthy relationships, and navigate the challenges of BPD. Consider therapies like Dialectical Behavior Therapy (DBT) or Cognitive Behavioral Therapy (CBT), which have proven effective in managing BPD symptoms.
- **Develop Mindfulness Practices:** Techniques like meditation and mindfulness can help you become more aware of your thoughts and emotions without judgment. This allows you to detach from overwhelming feelings and respond more rationally.
- **Join a Support Group:** Connecting with others who understand your struggles can be incredibly validating and encouraging. Support groups can provide a safe space to share experiences and learn from others.

Building a Strong Support System

Surrounding yourself with supportive and understanding people is crucial for managing BPD. Here's how to build a robust support system:

- **Identify Supportive People:** Seek out friends and family members who are understanding, patient, and accepting. Prioritize relationships built on trust, respect, and empathy.
- **Communicate Effectively:** Learn to express your needs and emotions assertively. Practice active listening skills to understand others better.
- **Set Healthy Boundaries:** Clear boundaries in relationships prevent resentment and foster mutual respect. Don't expect others to fill the void left by a genetic predisposition.

Remember:

- *Progress not Perfection: Learning to manage BPD is a journey, not a destination. There will be setbacks, but consistency is critical. Celebrate small victories and acknowledge your progress in building resilience.*
- *Self-compassion is Essential: Be kind to yourself. A genetic predisposition doesn't define you. Forgive yourself for past mistakes and focus on building a brighter future.*
- *Knowledge is Power: Educating yourself about the genetic aspects of BPD empowers you to take control of your treatment and build resilience. The more you understand your challenges, the better equipped you are to manage them.*

By understanding the potential role of genetics and taking proactive steps to manage your mental health, you can build resilience and thrive despite a genetic predisposition to BPD. Remember, you are not alone in this journey, and with the right tools and support, you can create a fulfilling life.

II- Understanding The Environmental Factors; The Scars That Shape Us: Healing from Adverse Childhood Experiences (ACEs) and Borderline Personality Disorder;

While the exact cause of BPD remains unknown, research suggests a strong link between **adverse childhood experiences (ACEs)** and its development. This chapter explores how these experiences can impact individuals with BPD and equips you with practical strategies for healing and building a brighter future.

Understanding the Impact of Adverse Childhood Experiences
Adverse childhood experiences (ACEs) encompass a wide range of traumatic experiences in childhood, that affects immensely on the personality of a person. Impact of ACE includes the following:

- **Physical or Sexual Abuse:** These experiences create a sense of fear and insecurity, making it difficult to trust others and develop healthy emotional regulation skills.
- **Emotional neglect:** Not receiving love, support, or validation during childhood can lead to low self-esteem, difficulty

identifying emotions, and a distorted sense of self-worth.
- **Unstable family environments:** Witnessing domestic violence, parental substance abuse, or frequent family conflict creates an unpredictable environment, leading to problems with emotional control and forming healthy relationships.

How do Adverse Childhood Experiences (ACEs) Shape BPD Symptoms?

Adverse childhood experiences (ACEs) can disrupt the normal development of emotional and social skills, contributing to BPD symptoms in several ways:

- **Disrupted Emotional Regulation:** Trauma can impair the development of healthy coping mechanisms for managing emotions. This can lead to intense emotional reactions and difficulty regulating them effectively.
- **Fragile Self-Identity:** Abuse and neglect can damage a child's sense of self-worth and identity. Individuals with BPD often struggle with a sense of emptiness and a distorted self-image.
- **Fearful Attachment Patterns:** ACEs can lead to insecure attachment styles characterized by a constant fear of abandonment or a desperate need for intimacy. This can significantly impact an individual's ability to build stable and healthy relationships.

Learning To Break the Cycle: Healing from Adverse Childhood Experiences (ACEs) and Building Resilience

The good news is that even with a history of ACEs, you can heal and build resilience in the face of BPD. Here are some practical steps you can take:

- **Acknowledge and Validate Your Pain:** The first step to healing is acknowledging the impact of your ACEs. Talking to a therapist or trusted friend can help you process these experiences and move forward.
- **Develop Self-Compassion:** Be kind to yourself. ACEs were not your fault, and healing takes time. Practice self-compassion and forgive yourself for negative behaviors or beliefs shaped by past experiences.
- **Identify Your Triggers:** Recognize situations or behaviors that trigger intense emotions or memories of your ACEs. This self-awareness empowers you to develop coping mechanisms for managing these triggers.

Building a Toolbox for Healing

Here are some specific tools and techniques that can be helpful in your healing journey:

- **Therapy:** Therapy provides a safe space to explore your past trauma and develop coping mechanisms. Therapies like Cognitive Behavioral Therapy (CBT) and Dialectical Behavior Therapy (DBT) can be particularly effective in managing BPD symptoms.
- **Journaling:** Writing down your thoughts and feelings can be a powerful tool for self-exploration and emotional processing. Journaling can help you identify unhelpful thought patterns and develop healthier coping methods.

- **Meditation and Mindfulness:** Mindfulness practices can help you become more aware of your thoughts and emotions without judgment. This allows you to detach from overwhelming feelings and respond more rationally.
- **Support Groups:** Connecting with others who understand your struggles can be incredibly validating and encouraging. Support groups can provide a safe space to share experiences and learn from others.

Building Healthy Relationships

Adverse childhood experiences (ACEs) can make it challenging to form healthy relationships. However, with effort, you can develop strong and supportive connections:

- **Set Healthy Boundaries:** Learn to say no and communicate your needs assertively. Having healthy boundaries prevents resentment and fosters mutual respect in your relationships.
- **Practice Effective Communication:** Clearly express your feelings and needs. Practice active listening skills to understand others better.
- **Choose Supportive People:** Surround yourself with people who accept and value you for who you are. Prioritize relationships that are built on trust, respect, and understanding.

Remember:

- ***Healing is a Journey:*** *Don't be discouraged by setbacks. Heal-*

*ing from trauma and managing BPD takes time and consis-
tent effort. Celebrate small victories and acknowledge your
progress.*

- ***Self-Care is Essential:*** *Prioritizing self-care activities is crucial
for physical and emotional well-being. Get enough sleep, eat
healthy meals, and engage in activities you enjoy.*
- ***Empowerment Through Knowledge:*** *Educating yourself about
ACEs and BPD allows you to take control of your treatment and
build resilience. The more you understand your challenges, the
better equipped you are to manage them by acknowledging the
impact of ACEs,*

III- Understanding Neurobiological Factors; When the Brain Speaks a Different Language: Understanding the Neurobiology of BPD and Strategies for Managing It

Borderline Personality Disorder (BPD) is a complex condition characterized by intense emotions, unstable relationships, and a distorted self-image. While the exact cause of BPD remains unknown, recent research has shed light on the potential role of neurobiological factors. This chapter explores how differences in brain structure, function, and neurotransmitters might contribute to BPD and equips you with practical strategies to manage these challenges.

The Symphony of the Brain: Understanding the Neurobiology of BPD

Our brains are like complex orchestras, with different regions working together to manage emotions, thoughts, and behaviors. Research suggests that in BPD, particular areas of this orchestra may be out of tune:

- **The Amygdala:** This region plays a crucial role in processing emotions, particularly fear and anger. Studies suggest that individuals with BPD may have an overactive amygdala, leading to heightened emotional responses to perceived threats or slights.
- **The Prefrontal Cortex (PFC) controls impulse control, planning, and decision-making. BPD research suggests potential dysfunction in the PFC, which could contribute** to impulsive behaviors and difficulty regulating emotions.
- **The Anterior Cingulate Cortex (ACC):** The ACC plays a role in emotional regulation, self-awareness, and empathy. Dysfunction in this area might contribute to the difficulties individuals with BPD face in experiencing and understanding their own emotions and those of others.

Chemical Messengers: Neurotransmitters and BPD

Neurotransmitters are chemical messengers in the brain that influence mood, behavior, and cognition. Research suggests that imbalances in certain neurotransmitters may be linked to BPD:

- **Serotonin:** Serotonin plays a role in regulating mood, sleep, and impulsivity. Lower levels of serotonin might contribute to mood swings, impulsivity, and difficulty coping with stress, common symptoms of BPD.
- **Dopamine:** Dopamine is associated with motivation, reward, and pleasure. Dysregulation of dopamine might contribute to the intense need for validation and the tendency to engage in risky behaviors observed in some individuals with BPD.

Understanding Doesn't Equal Curing, But It Empowers

While these neurobiological factors might contribute to BPD, it's important to remember that the brain is remarkably plastic. Here's how this understanding empowers you to manage your BPD:

- **Mindfulness and Emotional Regulation:** Techniques like mindfulness meditation can help you become more aware of your emotions and develop healthy coping mechanisms. Engaging in activities that promote relaxation, like deep breathing or yoga, can also help regulate your emotional state.
- **Building Emotional Vocabulary:** A rich vocabulary for your emotions allows you to express yourself more effectively and helps you manage overwhelming feelings. Therapy can help you develop this skill.
- **Challenging Negative Thoughts:** Our thoughts significantly influence our emotions and behaviors. When triggered, negative thoughts often take center stage. Learn to identify and challenge these thoughts with evidence-based

reasoning. Cognitive Behavioral Therapy (CBT) is beneficial for this.

Strategies for a More Balanced Brain Symphony

Here are some additional practical tips to manage the challenges posed by the neurobiological aspects of BPD:

- **Develop Healthy Habits:** Regular sleep, balanced meals, and exercise are crucial for promoting brain health and emotional well-being. Prioritize these activities for a more balanced brain chemistry.
- **Limit Substance Abuse:** Drugs and alcohol can further disrupt brain chemistry and worsen BPD symptoms. Seek professional help if you struggle with substance abuse.
- **Therapy is Key:** A therapist specializing in BPD can provide crucial support and guidance. Therapy can equip you with skills to manage emotions, build healthy relationships, and navigate the challenges of BPD.

Remember:

- **Progress, Not Perfection:** Learning to manage BPD is a journey, not a destination. There will be setbacks, but consistency is critical. Celebrate small victories and acknowledge your progress.
- **Self-Compassion is Your Ally:** Be kind to yourself. BPD is a complex condition, and change takes time. Forgive yourself for setbacks and utilize them as learning experiences.
- **Knowledge is Power:** By understanding the neurobiology

of BPD, you gain valuable insight into your challenges. This empowers you to make informed decisions about your treatment and management strategies.

The Takeaway: A Symphony Can Still Be Beautiful with a Few Off-Key Notes

BPD can be challenging, but understanding the potential role of neurobiological factors doesn't have to be discouraging. This knowledge empowers you to take control of your treatment and implement strategies to manage your symptoms. By incorporating these tips, developing self-awareness, and seeking professional support, you can learn to play a beautiful symphony with your brain, even if there are a few off-key notes.

IV- Understanding Invalidating Environments; The Echo Chamber of Invalidation: Healing from an Emotionally Stifling Childhood and Building Emotional Intelligence in BPD;

Borderline Personality Disorder (BPD) is a complex condition characterized by intense emotions, unstable relationships, and a distorted self-image. While the exact cause of BPD remains unknown, research suggests that growing up in an invalidating environment plays a significant role. **This chapter explores how childhood invalidation can contribute to BPD** and equips you with practical strategies to reclaim your emotional voice, build emotional intelligence, and create healthier relationships.

Understanding the Impact of Invalidation

An invalidating environment is one where your emotions and experiences are consistent:

- **Ignored:** Your caregivers fail to acknowledge your feelings or minimize their significance. ("You're overreacting!")
- **Dismissed:** Your thoughts and feelings are brushed aside or deemed unimportant. ("Don't be so dramatic.")
- **Judged:** You're shamed or criticized for expressing your emotions. ("Why are you always so sensitive?")

These experiences can have a profound impact on a developing child:

- **Difficulty Identifying Emotions:** When your emotions are constantly invalidated, it becomes difficult to identify and understand your feelings. This can lead to emotional confusion and difficulty expressing yourself effectively.
- **Heightened Sensitivity to Rejection:** Even mild criticism can feel like a devastating rejection if your emotions are never validated. This can contribute to a constant fear of abandonment, a core symptom of BPD.
- **Distorted Self-Image:** Chronic invalidation can damage your sense of self-worth and identity. You may question your perceptions and struggle with feelings of emptiness or worthlessness.

Breaking the Cycle: Reclaiming Your Emotional Voice

The good news is that even if you grew up in an invalidating environment, you can heal and build emotional intelligence. Here are some practical steps you can take:

- **Acknowledge the Impact:** Recognize how childhood invalidation has shaped your current struggles. Validate your own emotions and experiences.
- **Validate Yourself:** Start practicing self-validation. When you experience an emotion, acknowledge it and give it a name. (For example, "I feel angry because...") This helps you understand your feelings and healthily respond to them.
- **Challenge Negative Thoughts:** Invalidation can lead to

negative self-talk. Learn to identify and challenge these thoughts with evidence-based reasoning. Therapy like Cognitive Behavioral Therapy (CBT) can be beneficial in this process.

Building Emotional Intelligence

Emotional intelligence (EQ) is the ability to understand, use, and manage your emotions healthily. Here are some ways to improve your EQ:

- **Mindfulness Practices:** Techniques like meditation and journaling can help you become more aware of your thoughts and emotions without judgment. This allows you to observe your emotions and choose healthy responses.
- **Identify Your Triggers:** Recognize situations or behaviors that trigger intense emotions or memories of invalidation. Develop coping mechanisms to manage these triggers effectively.
- **Develop Healthy Emotional Vocabulary:** Having a rich vocabulary for your emotions allows you to express yourself more effectively and navigate complex emotional states.
- **Practice Emotional Regulation Skills:** Learn healthy coping mechanisms to manage difficult emotions. Techniques like deep breathing, relaxation exercises, and creative outlets can be helpful.

Building Supportive Relationships

One of the most challenging aspects of BPD is building healthy relationships. Here are some tips for navigating this:

- **Communicate Effectively:** Learn to express your needs and emotions assertively. Practice active listening skills to understand others better.
- **Set Healthy Boundaries:** Identify and set clear boundaries in your relationships. This prevents resentment and fosters mutual respect. Don't expect others to fill the emotional void left by childhood invalidation.
- **Seek Supportive People:** Surround yourself with people who validate your emotions and accept you for who you are. Prioritize relationships built on trust, respect, and empathy.

Remember:

- *Healing is a Journey: Don't be discouraged by setbacks. Healing takes time and consistent effort. Celebrate small victories and acknowledge your progress in reclaiming your emotional voice.*
- *Self-compassion is Key: Be kind to yourself. Childhood invalidation was not your fault, and healing takes time. Forgive yourself for past negative behaviors or beliefs shaped by past experiences.*
- *Knowledge is Power: Educating yourself about the impact of invalidation and BPD empowers you to take control of your treatment and build resilience. The more you understand your challenges, the better equipped you are to manage them.*

By acknowledging the impact of childhood invalidation, learning to validate yourself, and developing emotional intelligence, you can break the cycle and build a life filled with healthy relationships and emotional well-being. Remember, your voice matters, and you deserve to be heard.

6

The Symptoms and Subtype of Borderline Personality Disorder(BPD)

"You don't have to be positive all the time. Feeling sad, angry, annoyed, frustrated, scared, and anxious is okay. Having feelings doesn't make you a negative person. It makes you human." —
Lori Deschene.

Symptoms of BPD typically emerge during the teenage years and can vary from person to person. However, most individuals with BPD will experience at least five of the following symptoms over time:

- A pattern of severe mood changes over hours or days
- Extreme anger and problems controlling anger
- Strong, up-and-down relationships with family and friends, ranging from extreme closeness to anger and hostility
- Severe fear of abandonment and engaging in extreme

behaviors to avoid abandonment
- A rapidly changing sense of self that can cause sudden changes in goals, values, or behaviors
- Feeling disconnected from oneself, one's body, or reality, or experiencing paranoid thoughts
- Ongoing feelings of emptiness
- Self-destructive behaviors, such as substance use or misuse, binge eating, unsafe sex with multiple partners, dangerous driving, or reckless spending
- Suicide attempts or self-harming behavior, such as cutting, hair pulling, or burning

It's important to note that the symptoms of BPD may look like other medical conditions or problems. **Always talk with your healthcare provider for a proper and correct diagnosis.**

In addition to the symptoms above, it's essential to understand that a pattern of instability in emotions, self-image, and interpersonal relationships characterizes Borderline Personality Disorder (BPD). The symptoms of BPD can vary among individuals but typically fall into four main categories: emotional instability, disturbed self-image, impulsivity, and difficulties in relationships.

1. Emotional Instability:
Individuals with BPD often experience intense and rapidly shifting emotions, including difficulty regulating their emotions, leading to frequent and intense mood swings. These mood swings can range from anger, irritability, and anxiety to

sadness, emptiness, and feelings of worthlessness. Emotional dysregulation can also lead to self-harming behaviors, suicidal idealization, or attempts.

2. Disturbed Self-Image:

People with BPD often struggle with a distorted or unstable sense of self. They may have an unclear or shifting self-image and feel a chronic sense of emptiness. This can lead to identity confusion, difficulty making decisions, and not knowing who they are.

3. Impulsivity:

Impulsive behaviors are common in individuals with BPD. This can manifest in various ways, such as reckless driving, substance abuse, binge eating, overspending, or engaging in unsafe sexual practices. These impulsive behaviors are often attempts to alleviate emotional distress or fill a void.

4. Difficulties in Relationships:

Individuals with BPD often have unstable and intense relationships characterized by extreme idealization and devaluation. They usually experience a profound fear of abandonment and may engage in extreme behaviors to avoid real or perceived rejection. This fear of abandonment can lead to clingy or dependent behavior and intense anger or hostility towards others. Trust issues, a tendency to interpret neutral or ambiguous actions as unfavorable, and difficulties with boundaries are also common in BPD.

Subtypes of BPD Behavior

In addition to these core symptoms, there are also sub-types of BPD that have been identified based on patterns of behavior:

1. Impulsive Type: Individuals with this subtype exhibit the characteristics of impulsiveness and self-destructive behaviors, such as substance abuse, reckless driving, or self-harm.

2. Petulant Type: This subtype is characterized by chronic feelings of emptiness, irritability, and a tendency to engage in passive-aggressive behaviors.

3. Self-Destructive Type: People with this subtype of behavior often resort to self-harming as a way to cope with emotional pain.

4. Discouraged Type: This subtype is characterized by hopelessness, low self-esteem, and a tendency to withdraw from social interactions.

It's important to note that individuals with BPD may exhibit symptoms from multiple subtypes, and the presentation of symptoms can vary over time. A comprehensive assessment by a mental health therapist will only provide an accurate diagnosis and appropriate treatment.

MOST IMPORTANTLY:
Identifying emotional triggers that negatively affect relationships, the most critical aspect of learning to control and manage

one's behavior. This will help one lead a life that is as good as usual.

In next three chapters we will talk in great length about the how Borderline Personality Disorder affects our relationships whether in family, love relational or office relationships followed by HALLMARK SYMPTOM of BPD ;THE FEAR OF ABANDONMENT.

$$7$$

Difficulty In Relationship; Understanding Borderline Personality Disorder The Impact of BPD on Relationships

Borderline Personality Disorder (BPD) can have a significant impact on relationships, both romantic and non-romantic. The intense emotions, impulsivity, and fear of abandonment associated with BPD can create challenges and strain on interpersonal connections. Here are some ways BPD can affect relationships:

1. **Intense and Unstable Relationships**: BPD people often have intense and unstable relationships characterized by extreme idealization and devaluation. They may idolize their partner one moment and then quickly shift to seeing them as entirely negative. Such can lead to a roller coaster of emotions and confusion for both parties.

2. **Fear of Abandonment**: Individuals with Borderline Personality Disorder (BPD) often harbor an acute, though hidden, fear

of abandonment. This fear can show in various ways, such as clinginess, possessiveness, or a constant need for reassurance.

This fear can lead to the person with BPD becoming overly dependent on their partner, which can be overwhelming and suffocating for the other person.

3. Emotional Dysregulation: Individuals with BPD may struggle with regulating their emotions, leading to frequent and intense mood swings. This can make it very challenging for partners to understand and find the right way to respond to their emotional needs. The person with BPD may also struggle to communicate their emotions effectively, leading to misunderstandings and conflicts.

4. Impulsive Behaviors: Impulsivity is a prevalent trait in individuals with BPD, presenting itself in various ways, such as reckless spending, substance abuse, or engaging in risky sexual behaviors. These impulsive actions often strain relationships, resulting in financial hardships, trust issues, or emotional turmoil for both parties involved.

5. Idealization and Devaluation: The tendency to idealize and devalue others can create a turbulent relationship dynamic. In the idealization phase, individuals with BPD may elevate their partner to a pedestal, seeing them as perfect and meeting all their needs. However, during the devaluation phase, they may suddenly see their partner as flawed, unworthy, or abusive. This rapid shift in perception can be confusing and hurtful for the partner.

6. Boundary Issues: People with BPD may struggle with establishing and respecting boundaries within relationships. They may have difficulty discerning the line between themselves and their partner, potentially resulting in enmeshment or codependency. Alternatively, they may have rigid boundaries as a way to protect themselves from perceived abandonment, making it challenging for their partner to connect with them on an emotional level.

7. **Communication Challenges**: Difficulties in effectively communicating emotions and needs can strain relationships. The person with BPD may struggle to express themselves calmly and coherently, leading to misunderstandings and conflicts. They may also tend to interpret neutral or ambiguous actions as harmful, leading to frequent arguments or feelings of rejection.

It's important to note that the combination of appropriate treatment, such as therapy and medication, can empower individuals with BPD to manage their symptoms and foster healthier relationships effectively. Open and honest communication, setting boundaries, and seeking support from mental health professionals can help both individuals in the relationship navigate the challenges posed by BPD.

8

Fear Of Abandonment- A HALLMARK SYMPTOM of Borderline Personality Disorder: Conquering Fear of Abandonment and Building Secure Relationships

In this chapter, we will delve deeply into another **critical aspect** of BPD: the intense fear of abandonment and its associated challenges that individuals with BPD encounter in establishing and sustaining healthy relationships. This chapter will explore the root causes of this fear, provide practical management techniques, and offer guidance on cultivating trust, effective communication, and establishing healthy boundaries to mitigate the risk of extreme actions such as suicide resulting from relationship failures.

The fear of abandonment is perhaps the most defining characteristic of Borderline Personality Disorder (BPD). It's a pervasive anxiety that someone you care about will leave you, be it through a breakup, a perceived slight, or even a temporary physical separation. This fear can manifest in many ways, often leading to intense emotions, impulsive behaviors, and strained relationships.

Let's delve into the roots of abandonment fear in BPD, explore its impact, and, most importantly, equip you with tools and strategies to overcome it.

Understanding the Origins:

The fear of abandonment often stems from early childhood experiences of neglect, abuse, or unpredictable caregiver relationships. These experiences can create a core belief that you are unlovable or unworthy, leaving you constantly seeking validation and fearing rejection. Additionally, individuals with BPD may have a heightened sensitivity to perceived slights or changes in behavior, misinterpreting them as signs of imminent abandonment.

Reasons for Fear of Abandonment:

- **Early life experiences:** Unreliable caregivers, emotional neglect, or past experiences of abandonment can trigger this fear.
- **Black and white thinking:** Viewing situations in extremes (all good or all bad) can lead to the belief that any disagreement or separation signifies the end of the relationship.
- **Emotional dysregulation:** Intense emotions can make individuals with BPD **misinterpret actions or communication**, leading to feelings of rejection.

The Impact of This Constant Fear Of Abandonment:

This constant fear can have a significant impact on various aspects of life:

- **Relationships:** The fear can lead to clingy behavior, possessiveness, and intense jealousy. It can also make it difficult to trust others and develop healthy emotional intimacy.
- **Emotions:** The fear can trigger intense emotions like anxiety, anger, and sadness. These emotions can further strain relationships and lead to impulsive behaviors like self-harm or substance abuse.
- **Self-Esteem:** The fear of being unlovable can contribute to low self-esteem and a distorted sense of self-worth.

Techniques for Managing Fear:

- **Mindfulness practices:** Techniques like meditation and deep breathing can help regulate emotions and gain perspective in situations that trigger abandonment fears.
- **Cognitive Behavioral Therapy (CBT):** CBT helps identify and challenge negative thought patterns associated with abandonment.
- **Distraction techniques:** Engaging in healthy activities during intense fear can help manage overwhelming emotions.
- **Building self-worth:** Focusing on personal strengths and developing healthy self-esteem can reduce dependence on external validation.

Building Trust:

- **Open and honest communication:** Sharing feelings openly and actively listening to your partner can foster trust and understanding.
- **Reliability and consistency:** Following through on commitments and demonstrating consistent behavior builds trust over time.
- **Setting realistic expectations:** Communicating your needs and understanding your partner's limitations can build trust and prevent misunderstandings.

Fostering Healthy Communication:

- **"I" statements:** Using "I" statements allows for clear communication of feelings and avoids accusatory language.
- **Active listening:** Pay close attention to your partner, validate their feelings, and avoid interrupting.
- **Expressing appreciation:** Acknowledging your partner's efforts and expressing gratitude strengthens the bond.

Setting Boundaries:

- **Identifying your needs:** Understand your emotional boundaries and what you are comfortable with in a relationship.
- **Communicating boundaries clearly:** Express your needs calmly and assertively.
- **Respecting others' boundaries:** It is crucial to be mindful of your partner's boundaries and their limitations.

I trust that readers will be able to recognize these signs in their personalities and take proactive steps to address and improve themselves. If they encounter difficulties, I encourage them to seek medical assistance promptly to facilitate resolution and promote personal growth and well-being.

Few practical Self Help Strategies to manage the Crippling fear of abandonment;

Based on the above, the following can be summarized as self-help strategies;

Identify Your Triggers:
The first step is understanding what triggers your abandonment anxiety. To understand the triggers, you can use the following:

- **Recording/Journaling:** Track situations that evoke intense fear of abandonment. Analyze patterns. Was it a perceived slight from a friend, a partner's late reply, or a canceled social event? Recognizing these triggers is crucial for applying self-help strategies effectively.
- **Challenging Negative Thoughts:** Negative thought patterns often fuel abandonment anxiety. When a trigger is activated, these thoughts might scream, "They're going to leave you!" or "You're not good enough." Challenge these thoughts! Ask yourself if there is concrete evidence to support these beliefs. Could there be a more realistic explanation for the situation?

Building Emotional Awareness:
Mindfulness practices are powerful tools to manage emotions effectively.

- **Deep Breathing:** When triggered, practice deep breathing exercises. Inhale slowly through your nose for a count of 4, hold for 7 seconds, and exhale slowly through your mouth for a count of 8. Repeat this for a few minutes. Focus on the physical sensations of your breath and release tension with each exhalation.
- **Mindful Observation:** Observe your emotions without judgment. Acknowledge the fear, but don't identify with it. Imagine yourself watching your thoughts and feelings like passing clouds in the sky.

Developing Secure Attachment

BPD often stems from early experiences of insecure attachment. While not a quick fix, fostering secure attachment patterns can help ease abandonment anxiety.

- **Focus on Healthy Relationships:** Identify supportive people who accept you for who you are. Nurture these relationships by engaging in quality time and practicing effective communication.
- **Develop a Strong Support System:** Build a network of friends, family members, or a therapist who can provide emotional support and reassurance. Consider joining a BPD support group to connect with others who understand your struggles.

Prioritizing Self-Care:

Taking care of yourself is vital for emotional resilience.

- **Maintain Healthy Habits:** Prioritize enough sleep, eat nutritious meals, and exercise regularly. These habits improve your overall well-being and emotional regulation.
- **Engage in Activities You Enjoy:** Make time for hobbies and activities that bring you joy and a sense of accomplishment. This boosts your self-esteem and reduces dependence on others for validation.

Setting Healthy Boundaries:

Boundaries are crucial in healthy relationships. Learn to say no and communicate your needs assertively. This prevents resentment and fosters mutual respect. Don't be afraid to express your desire for connection, but don't make it a demand that triggers abandonment fears if not met immediately.

Remember:

- ***Progress, Not Perfection:*** *Learning to manage abandonment anxiety is a journey, not a destination. There will be setbacks, but consistency is critical. Celebrate your progress, no matter how small.*
- ***Self-compassion is Essential:*** *Be kind to yourself. Acknowledge that change takes time and effort. Forgive yourself for setbacks and use them as learning experiences.*
- ***Seek Professional Help:*** *Consider therapy specializing in BPD. A therapist can provide individualized support, teach specific coping mechanisms, and help you navigate the underlying causes of your fear.*

By actively implementing these self-help strategies, you can gradually loosen the grip of abandonment anxiety. Remember, you are worthy of love and healthy relationships. You can build a fulfilling life rooted in self-compassion, emotional regulation, and secure attachments.

9

Borderline Personality Disorder and it's Impact on Various Type Of Relationships

You are not alone. You are seen. I am with you. You are not alone."
— Shonda Rhimes.

Borderline personality disorder (BPD) can have a significant impact on various relationships. An individual with BPD often struggles with intense emotions, difficulty regulating their feelings, and a fear of abandonment. These challenges can make it challenging for them to maintain stable and healthy relationships. Here are some ways BPD can affect different types of relationships:

1. **Romantic Relationships:** BPD can lead to intense and unstable relationships characterized by extreme highs and

lows. People with BPD may fear abandonment and become overly dependent on their partners, leading to clinginess and possessiveness. They may also experience intense jealousy and tend to idealize or devalue their partners.

2. Family Relationships: BPD can also strain relationships with family members. Individuals with BPD may have difficulty managing conflicts, and they may engage in impulsive behaviors that can be distressing for their loved ones. They may also struggle with trust and fear rejection, impacting their ability to maintain healthy connections with family members.

3. Friendships: BPD can make it challenging to maintain stable friendships. People with BPD may have difficulty with boundaries, leading to intense and unpredictable emotional reactions. They may also struggle with self-identity, causing them to feel insecure and seek validation from others, which can strain friendships.

4. Professional Relationships: BPD can impact professional relationships as well. People with BPD may struggle with emotional regulation, leading to difficulties in managing stress and conflicts in the workplace. They may also fear rejection or criticism, making it challenging to receive feedback or work collaboratively with colleagues.

To Recapitulate above, Borderline Personality Disorder has its Impact on;

It's important to note that while BPD can present challenges in relationships, individuals with BPD mostly learn to manage their symptoms and develop healthier relationship patterns by taking proper treatment, guidance, and support. Dialectical behavior therapy (DBT) can also be beneficial in improving relationship skills and emotional regulation for individuals with BPD.

10

Preparing for Treatment: Gearing Yourself and Family and Friends Up To Move Forward

- *"Life doesn't make any sense without interdependence. We need each other, and the sooner we learn that, the better for us all." —Erik Erikson.*

This chapter discusses the steps that you, your family, and your friends should take before treatment commences.

Coping with BPD can pose significant challenges, but it's essential to remember that help is available. Whether it's you, a family member, or a friend who is grappling with BPD, this book, "Breaking the Silence: Illuminating the Intricacies of

Borderline Personality Disorder and Its Profound Influence On Relationships," is designed to offer awareness, guidance, support, and valuable information about community resources for you and your loved ones.

First Step: Learning To Help Yourself;

Individually, a person with BPD may acknowledge the harmful nature of their behavior yet struggle to exert control over it. Proper treatment is essential for managing these challenges effectively. Here are several alternative approaches to self-help:

- **You are connecting with others.** Engage in open conversations and share your fears and thoughts about BPD to seek emotional support from individuals who are also navigating the condition. Joining groups on social media platforms can provide valuable connections and be a helpful tool. This will help you share your notes /situations with others and find ways to normalize yourself.
- **Eat correctly and exercise well.**
- **Try meditation, yoga, or Tai Chi**.
- **Avoid alcohol or drugs:** Refrain from consuming alcohol or drugs as they can significantly harm your well-being, disrupt emotional balance, and interfere with the effectiveness of medications.

Second Step: Helping & Supporting A Family Member Or Friend

For individuals with BPD, the support of family and friends is paramount in their treatment journey. This support helps individuals with BPD stay connected with their loved ones, preventing them from isolating themselves from relationships, which are vital for their well-being.

- Each family member needs to keep watch on the erratic behaviors of a BPD family person. Erratic behavior includes going for sudden shopping sprees, indulging in sexual or substance binges, and or getting into sudden fighting/arguing. If possible, engage your loved one to discuss their behaviors with them and make them identify these signs as early detection.

- Family and friends must encourage and convince family members with BPD to seek proper treatment, offering them hope for relief from their complex and often frustrating illness.

- Help them understand the importance of treatment. If a loved one is taking a skills-based approach to DBT, learn the language of this treatment to help provide support to your loved ones.

- Always speak honestly and kindly. Don't ridicule your friend or family member, as such behavior may lead your BPD person to lose control of their behavior, thereby forcing them to resort to bad choices. Instead, make offers of help and show them that person who cares about them. Ask how they're feeling.

- Always react calmly. Even when your family member or friend is in crisis, make sure you remain calm and listen and make them feel understood, then take the next step toward getting help.

Third Step: Helping Children When You Notice Symptoms

Suppose you strongly suspect that your child is exhibiting symptoms of BPD. In that case, taking immediate action is crucial to persuading your child to schedule an appointment with a licensed psychiatrist or psychologist. Contacting your regular pediatrician or primary care physician is the next step if this proves challenging. During the consultation, ensure you provide comprehensive details regarding the symptoms and behaviors observed in your child, including the details given as under:

- Evaluations of past mental health and available other medical records
- Describing all the symptoms you are noticing and since when.
- Details of medications or other medical treatments the child has been prescribed.
- Also, provide any other information asked for by the doctor, physician, or anything else that the psychiatrist or psychologist requests.

If you disagree with the conclusions of a doctor, physician, psychiatrist, or psychologist, it is always advisable to get a second opinion. It is always better to remain cautious than ignore a severe problem.

If your child ever reports seeing or hearing things that are not there, that too without being under the influence of drugs or alcohol, then you should seek medical treatment immediately. This may be an episode of psychosis. Such episodes might also include:

- *Spontaneous violent behavior.*
- *Denial of reality.*
- *These nonsensical and paranoid claims.*
- *Removal of clothing.*
- *Reckless and dangerous behavior.*

- *Claims of invincibility and other special powers.*

11

"Handling Emergency Situations: Calling 911"

"There is hope, even when your brain tells you there isn't." — **John Green.**

Sometimes, the home situation gets into a crisis; at this stage, you may be forced to call the Police. Think twice, as such an action negatively affects your child or relative tremendously. Thankfully, there are some steps you can take to keep the situation as calm as possible.

On the phone: Firstly, it's the responsibility of family or friends of a person with BPD to share details of the individual's current situation with the 911 operator.

Explain to the dispatcher the mental health situation your loved one is experiencing in detail. It's crucial to apprise them of the mental health crisis unfolding clearly. Remember, if the Police at the location are not fully informed about the mental health crisis, the dispatcher may not be able to handle the situation appropriately. Providing comprehensive information is essential for ensuring the safety and well-being of your loved one. In many communities, there exist **Crisis Intervention Team (CIT) programs** under which police officers are trained to respond to and handle such psychiatric crisis calls. It would help if you always preferred to ask for a CIT officer.

During a crisis, Police are trained to maintain control and ensure safety. If you are worried that police officers may overreact, the best thing to do is to remain calm in such a situation. As a police officer arrives at your home, say, "This is a mental health crisis." You can share helpful information and step aside and out of the way. Yelling or getting too close to the officer will likely make him feel out of control. You want the officer to be as calm as possible.

The family of a person with BPD should be prepared for the possibility that during this process, their loved one may be handcuffed and transported in the back of a police car. This can be a distressing sight to witness, and it's important to anticipate potential backlash from the individual with BPD as a result.

What Can the Police Do?

Police can move/transport individuals who require hospital care and are willing to go voluntarily. A well-trained Crisis Intervention Team (CIT) officer within the police department is often equipped to communicate with and de-escalate agitated individuals, persuading them to seek treatment at the hospital voluntarily.

Also, if involuntary, Police can take a person to a hospital for an evaluation. If needed under certain circumstances, Police can resort to the forced evacuation of a person in crisis to the hospital for a mental health evaluation involuntarily. Here, laws vary from state to state.

In summary, always be vigilant about the welfare of your family members. There may be a situation where you are worried about them but can't reach them for some reason. Use the facility available to Police by calling the non-emergency number in your area/community and explaining your concern. Ask them to conduct a welfare check.

Information on some of The Hotlines:

In addition to the above, information on various hotlines is given as follows;

- **National Suicide Prevention Lifeline:** 988 - Offers 24/7, accessible, and confidential support for people in distress, as well as prevention and crisis resources for you or your loved ones.
- **Crisis Text Line:** Text HOME to 741741 to connect with a crisis counselor via text message.
- **The Trevor Project:** 1-866-488-7386 - Provides crisis intervention and suicide prevention services specifically for LGBTQ+ youth.

Life might feel like it's an unrelenting crisis or emergency at times.

Suppose you have a diagnosis of borderline personality disorder and are feeling suicidal, self-injurious, or self-destructive. In that case, the good news is that some people are willing to help.

Whatever you are doing right now, stop and commit to keeping yourself safe and alive for the next hour.

I'm serious. Set the timer on your phone for 60 minutes. Promise yourself that you won't make any problems worse during that time. The truth is that even intense emotions and urges can change within an hour or two. You don't have to add to your pain or trauma. You don't have to hurt others.

Letting people know that you need help is always a smart decision. Keep telling others until they listen.

Suicide Prevention Lifeline

988

Warm Lines

These are peer-run organizations and may not be available 24/7.

Crisis Text Line

If you can't talk, text.

Samaritans NYC

1-212-673-3000

Veterans Crisis Line

1-800-273-8255 (Press 1) or text 838255

RAINN

Sexual assault hotline

1-800-656-4673

National Alliance on Mental Illness (NAMI) Crisis Text Line
Text 741741
Again, if you can't talk, text.

12

Treatment Options for Borderline Personality Disorder People

The advice I'd give to somebody silently struggling is that you don't have to live that way. You don't have to struggle in silence. You can be un-silent. You can live well with a mental health condition, as long as you open up to somebody about it because you must share your experience with people so that you can get the help that you need." —Demi Lovato.

In the United States, there are several treatment options available for individuals with Borderline Personality Disorder (BPD). Several research advanced associations are available in the US to treat personality disorders. However, treatment plans may vary from person to person, depending on the severity of the symptoms. Here are some commonly used treatment options:

Treatment Options For Borderline Personality Disorder People

1. **Psychotherapy Treatment**: Psychotherapy, particularly Dialectical Behavior Therapy (DBT), is considered the gold standard treatment in BPD cases.DBT focuses on teaching individuals efficient skills for managing intense emotions. It also focuses on improving interpersonal relationships and developing coping strategies. Individual therapy, group therapy, and skills training are essential components of DBT.

1. **Use Of Medication:** While there is no specific medication approved in the cases of BPD, certain drugs can used on a symptomatic basis to help manage depression, anxiety, or impulsivity. Psychiatrists prescribe medicines like antidepressants, mood stabilizers, and anti-psychotics to address these symptoms. Medication is often used in conjunction with psychotherapy.

1. **Mentalization-Based Therapy (MBT)**: MBT is another therapy approach that focuses on helping individuals with BPD develop a better understanding of both their thoughts and feelings and those of others. It aims to improve emotional regulation and interpersonal functioning.

1. **Schema-focused therapy:** This approach targets the underlying patterns and beliefs contributing to BPD symptoms. It helps individuals identify and change maladaptive schemas or core beliefs that drive their behavior and emotional reactions.

1. **Transference-Focused Psychotherapy (TFP):** TFP is a psycho-dynamic therapy that explores and understands the individual's internal world and relationships. It aims to help individuals with BPD to develop healthier ways of managing their emotions.

1. **Supportive Therapy:** Supportive therapy must provide a safe and non-judgmental space for individuals having BPD to express their emotions and concerns. It focuses on building a therapeutic alliance and providing emotional support.

It's always important to seek the help of a mental health professional, a psychiatrist, or a psychologist to determine the most appropriate treatment plan for an individual with BPD. Treatment may involve a combination of therapies tailored to the individual's needs. In addition, families can use self-help resources and support groups. Lifestyle changes can also be beneficial in combating BPD symptoms.

13

Living with BPD: Self-Care, Self-help and Coping Strategies

"The experience I have had is that once you start talking about [experiencing a mental health struggle], you realize that you're part of quite a big club." —Prince Harry

Understanding and implementing self-care strategies and coping mechanisms are crucial for both individuals dealing with BPD and their families. Living with Borderline Personality Disorder (BPD) can sometimes be very challenging. However, being aware of several self-care strategies and coping mechanisms will make the lives of family members more accessible, reduce their symptoms, and improve their overall well-being.

LIVING WITH BPD: SELF-CARE, SELF-HELP, AND COPING STRATEGIES

Self-care Strategies are:

Educate Yourself: Learning as much as possible about BPD will help you understand the Disorder. It can also help you make sense of your experiences and provide a foundation for effective self-care strategies.

Seek Professional Help: Work with a mental health professional specializing in BPD. They can provide guidance, support, and evidence-based treatments such as therapy and medication.

1. **Practice Mindfulness and Self-Awareness**: Mindfulness techniques include deep breathing exercises and meditation. These will help you become more aware of your emotions and thoughts, enabling you to respond to them more constructively and healthily.
2. **Develop Healthy Coping Skills:** These skills can be developed by identifying healthy coping mechanisms suitable for your temperament and can help you, such as engaging in hobbies, journalism, listening to music, or practicing relaxation techniques. These activities can significantly help you manage stress and regulate your emotions.
3. **Establish a Routine:** Schedule your activities by creating a structured daily routine, including all the personal and

official to-do lists. This step will provide stability and a sense of control and achievement. It can help you manage your time and significantly reduce anxiety.

4. **Build a Support Network:** Surround yourself with supportive and understanding individuals who can provide emotional support. Joining support groups or online communities is a great way to connect with others who share similar experiences.

5. **Set Boundaries:** Healthy boundaries are crucial in managing relationships. Communicate your needs and limits to others, and learn to say no when necessary.

6. **Practice Self-Compassion**: The success of the therapy is achieved by being kind to yourself and practicing self-compassion. Remind yourself that it's okay to have bad days and that you are doing your best.

7. **Take Care of Your Physical Health**: Regularly exercise, eat a balanced diet, and, most importantly, get enough sleep. Remember that physical health can significantly impact mental well-being.

8. **Avoid Substance Abuse**: Substance abuse can worsen BPD symptoms. It's important to avoid using drugs or alcohol as a means of coping.

Self-help techniques using Mindfulness activities

Some mindfulness techniques can also be incorporated into various aspects of daily life. The key is to bring your attention to the present moment without judgment and fully engage your senses. In Chapter 22, I will provide details on several mindful techniques with live examples.

Remember:

Self-care is a continuous journey; what works for one person may not work for another. It's essential to experiment with various strategies to discover what best suits your needs and adapt to the specific requirements of your treatment plan. Practice patience with yourself and acknowledge and celebrate even the most minor victories.

14

Few Critical Issues of Young Adults Borderline Personality Disorder; Handling Of Suicide, Social and Family Issues

"The experience I have had is that once you start talking about [experiencing a mental health struggle], you realize that you're part of quite a big club." — Prince Harry

Handling a Few Important Issues of Young & Adults with BPD On Suicide, Social and Family Issues ;

Many young adults with BPD face personal, family, or social challenges that they find exceedingly difficult to manage. These situations can often push individuals towards suicidal thoughts or actions.

Therefore, it's crucial to approach these issues with the utmost care, sensitivity, and attention. Thus, it's essential to approach the topic of suicidal feelings in individuals with Borderline Personality Disorder (BPD) with seriousness and accuracy. It is necessary for a person having BPD symptoms to learn to identify such symptoms & triggers within themselves. Triggers may vary from person to person.

The high prevalence and increased suicide rate in patients with BPD make an unassailable argument that effective treatment needs to be developed and that treatment has to be widely available.

While several treatments for BPD are moderately effective in randomized controlled trials, it remains of considerable concern that most of them require extensive training, making them unavailable to most patients. **Mentalization-based treatment (MBT)** was developed with this in mind. It requires relatively little additional training on top of general mental health training. It has been implemented in research studies by community mental health professionals, primarily nurses, with limited training given modest levels of supervision.

Identifying The Extreme Signals and Triggers;

The following are some common signs that a person with BPD is likely to experience:

1. Intense and rapidly shifting emotions, such as sadness, anger, or emptiness.
2. Feelings of hopelessness or worthlessness.
3. Impulsive behaviors, such as self-harm or substance abuse.
4. An intense fear of abandonment or rejection.
5. Chronic feelings of emptiness and a lack of identity.
6. Difficulty regulating emotions, leading to frequent mood swings.
7. You are engaging in risky behaviors or having a history of self-destructive actions.

It is also essential to note that not everyone with Borderline Personal Disorder will experience such extreme thoughts of suicide, and these signs can vary from person to person. However, if anyone exhibits three or more signs, it's crucial to take action by:

- *Consulting certified mental health professionals.*
- *Share your thoughts with groups of individuals with similar experiences to ensure accuracy and provide practical recommendations for prevention and support.*

Handling Family Issues;

Many young adults with Borderline Personality Disorder face extreme difficulty in handling family relationship issues that they find exceedingly difficult to manage. These situations can become so extreme that they often push individuals towards suicidal thoughts or actions.

Navigating through family issues can sometimes be challenging for individuals with borderline personality disorder (BPD). Following are some aspects to be focused on while handling family issues;

Navigating through family issues can sometimes be challenging for individuals with borderline personality disorder (BPD).

Here are some tips that may help:

1. Seek professional help: Consider working with a therapist or counselor specializing in BPD. They can provide guidance, support, and strategies for managing family dynamics.

2. Educate your family: Help your family members understand BPD by providing them with educational resources or encouraging them to attend therapy sessions with you. This can foster empathy, reduce stigma, and improve communication.

3. Practice effective communication: Learn and practice assertive communication skills to express your thoughts, feelings, and needs clearly. Encourage open and honest conversations with your family, promoting understanding and healthy dialogue.

4. Set boundaries: Establish and communicate your boundaries with your family. Let them know what is acceptable and what is not in terms of behavior, conversations, and interactions. Be firm in enforcing these boundaries to protect your well-being.

5. Manage emotional triggers: Identify specific situations or topics that trigger intense emotions and discuss them with your family. Collaborate on finding ways to minimize triggers and develop coping strategies together.

6. Practice self-care: Prioritize self-care activities that promote emotional well-being, such as exercise, mindfulness, hobbies, and spending time with supportive friends. Taking care of yourself is essential for managing family issues effectively.

7. Consider family therapy: Family therapy can improve communication, resolve conflicts, and strengthen relationships. It provides a safe space for everyone to express their feelings and work towards healthier dynamics.

Remember, each family situation is unique, and these tips may need to be tailored to your specific circumstances. It's essential to be patient with yourself and your family as you navigate these challenges.

Handling Social Issues;

Many young adults with Borderline Personality Disorder face extreme difficulty in handling social issues to the extent that they choose to be aloof than being part of a social /family circle . They find it extremely difficult to manage these social issues some time led them towards suicidal thoughts or actions.

Handling social issues, too, can be handled by the individuals with borderline personality disorder (BPD) with the help of some tips given as under;

Handling social issues, too, can be challenging for individuals with borderline personality disorder (BPD). Here are some tips that may help:

1. **Build a support network**: Surround yourself with understanding and supportive friends or loved ones who can provide emotional support. Supporting groups specific to BPD can also offer a sense of community and learning.

2. **Educate yourself and others:** Learn more about BPD and share information with those close to you. This can reduce stigma and increase understanding, fostering more supportive social interactions.

3. **Practice self-awareness**: Develop a better understanding of your emotions, triggers, and behavior patterns. This can help you manage your reactions and communicate more effectively in social situations.

4. **Develop coping strategies:** Identify healthy coping mechanisms that work for you, such as deep breathing exercises, grounding techniques, or engaging in activities that help regulate your emotions. Practice these strategies when faced with social challenges.

5. **Set realistic expectations:** Understand that not every social interaction will be perfect, and that's okay. Accept that there may be ups and downs, and focus on progress rather than perfection.

6. Communicate your needs: Be open and honest about your needs and boundaries in social situations. Clearly express what you're comfortable with and what you're not. Effective communication can help others understand and respect your limits.

7. Practice social skills: Improve your social skills through therapy, role-playing, or self-help resources. Effective communication, active listening, and conflict-resolution techniques can enhance social interactions.

8. Take breaks when needed: Recognize when you need to take breaks from social situations to recharge and prioritize self-care. It's okay to step back and focus on your well-being.

Remember, everyone's journey with BPD is unique, and it's essential to be patient and kind to yourself as you navigate social challenges. Seeking professional help from a therapist specializing in BPD can provide additional guidance and support.

15

Case Studies of Few BPD Persons in Different Situations

"I would say what others have said: It gets better. One day, you'll find your tribe. You have to trust that people are out there waiting to love you and celebrate you for who you are. In the meantime, you might have to be your tribe. You might have to be your own best friend. That's not something they're going to teach you in school. So start the work of loving yourself. — Wentworth Miller

Here are case studies of following individuals with borderline personality disorder (BPD), and going through their journey will help you know how they managed their crises:

Case Study -1:

The Case Study of Sarah-Struggling with Borderline Personality Disorder

The Case Study of Sarah

Let's take a look at the case study of Sarah (name changed), a US citizen who struggled with Borderline Personality Disorder (BPD) and managed to overcome her challenges.

Sarah's journey with BPD began in her early twenties. She experienced intense mood swings, had difficulty maintaining stable relationships, and often felt a deep sense of emptiness. Sarah's impulsive behaviors, such as reckless spending and substance abuse, further complicated her life. Her emotions were overwhelming, and she frequently conflicted with those around her.

Recognizing the need for help, Sarah sought professional assistance. She started attending therapy sessions with a licensed psychologist who specialized in treating BPD. Together, they embarked on a journey of healing and recovery.

Sarah's therapist introduced her to Dialectical Behavior Therapy (DBT), a treatment specifically designed for individuals with BPD. Through DBT, Sarah learned various skills to manage her emotions and improve her relationships. She practiced mindfulness techniques to ground herself in the present moment and regulate her intense emotions. Sarah also developed interpersonal effectiveness skills, which helped her communicate effectively and set healthy boundaries in her relationships.

In addition to therapy, Sarah also took medication to address her pronounced symptoms of depression and anxiety. This and treatment provided her with the necessary support to navigate her daily challenges.

Sarah's recovery was not without setbacks. She faced moments of relapse and struggled with the fear of abandonment. However, with the support of her therapist and a strong support network, she persevered.

Sarah also recognized the importance of self-care. Hence, she tried engaging in activities that brought her joy and helped her manage stress. Regular exercise, practicing hobbies, and spending time with loved ones became integral to her routine.

Over time, Sarah's dedication to therapy, medication, and self-care paid off. She began to experience more stability in her emotions and relationships. Sarah's impulsive behaviors reduced, and she better understood herself.

Today, Sarah leads a fulfilling life. She has developed a strong sense of self and can maintain healthy and stable relationships.

While she still faces occasional challenges, Sarah has built a toolbox of skills and strategies to manage them effectively.

Key Takeaways from Sarah's Story
Sarah's story highlights the importance of seeking professional help, engaging in therapy, and practicing self-care in the journey toward recovery from BPD. With the proper support and determination, individuals with BPD can overcome their challenges and lead fulfilling lives.

Case Study 2:

Julie's Journey Towards Impulse Control

Let's take a case study to explain. Here I share a case study of Julie (name changed), a person with BPD, and their experience with managing impulsive behaviors:

Julie is a 34-year-old woman diagnosed with Borderline Personality Disorder (BPD). She has struggled with impulsive behaviors throughout her life, often engaging in self-harm and risky activities. However, with therapy and support, Julie has made significant progress in managing her impulses.

Julie's journey began when she sought therapy after a challenging period in her life. Through treatment, she gained a better understanding of her emotions and learned various coping.

Strategies that helped Julie control her impulses:

1. **Dialectical Behavior Therapy (DBT)**: Julie participated in DBT, a type of therapy specifically designed for individuals with BPD. DBT taught her mindfulness, emotional regulation, distress tolerance, and interpersonal effectiveness skills. These skills helped her identify triggers, manage intense emotions, and make healthier choices.

1. **Building a Support Network**: Julie surrounded herself with a supportive network of friends, family, and mental health professionals who understood her condition. They encouraged her, understood her, and provided practical assistance during difficult times.

1. **Developing Safety Plans**: Julie worked with her therapist to create safety plans for moments when her impulses felt overwhelming. These plans included strategies like calling a trusted friend, engaging in grounding exercises, or distracting herself with a favorite hobby.

1. **Engaging in Healthy Outlets**: Julie discovered the importance of finding healthy emotional outlets. She started journalism, practicing yoga, and engaging in creative activities like painting. These outlets gave her a constructive way to express her emotions and reduce impulsive urges.

1. **Medication Management**: Julie worked closely with a psychiatrist to find the proper medication regimen to help manage her symptoms. Medication, in conjunction with therapy, helped stabilize her mood and reduce impulsive behaviors.

Over time, Julie's commitment to therapy, self-reflection, and utilizing these strategies helped her gain greater control over her impulses. Although she faced challenges, she developed the resilience and skills necessary to navigate her emotions and make healthier choices.

Key Takeaways from Julie's Story
Remember, this case study is to give a way to handle such situations, and it's essential to consult with mental health professionals and individuals with lived experiences to ensure accuracy and provide a well-rounded perspective in your book.

Case Study -3:

Case study of Mark's Path to Resilience

Mark, a 28-year-old man from New York, faced significant challenges due to his BPD. He struggled with impulsive behaviors, intense mood swings, and a fear of abandonment. However, through resilience and a commitment to self-improvement, Mark overcame his crises and built a fulfilling life.

Mark recognized the importance of therapy and began working with a BPD specialist. Through treatment, he gained insight into his emotional triggers and learned healthier ways to cope with stress. Mark also engaged in schema therapy, which helped him identify and challenge negative thought patterns that contributed to his crises.

To address his fear of abandonment, Mark joined a support group for individuals with BPD, which helped him connect with others who understood his experiences and provided a safe space for sharing and learning from one another. The support group became a valuable source of encouragement and validation for Mark.

In addition to therapy and support groups, Mark focused on developing his self-esteem and self-worth. He engaged in activities that nurtured his passions and talents, such as writing and volunteering. These activities helped him build a sense of purpose and confidence, reducing his reliance on external validation.

Mark's crises became less frequent and more manageable with time and consistent effort. He learned to recognize his triggers and implement healthy coping strategies, such as deep breathing and journalism. Mark's journey showcases the power of resilience, therapy, and self-development in overcoming crises and building a fulfilling life.

Key Takeaways from Mark's Story
These case studies highlight the transformative power of therapy, support, and self-care in managing crises and finding stability for individuals with BPD. They serve as inspiring examples for US citizens, demonstrating that with the right tools and support, it is possible to navigate the challenges of BPD and lead fulfilling lives.

Case Study -4:

Case study of Angel's Path to overcoming the fear of abandonment

The Case of Angel: A Journey of Healing

Angel, a 28-year-old artist, lived in a constant state of anxiety. Her relationships were turbulent, characterized by intense idealization followed by devastating breakups. Every perceived disagreement felt like a looming abandonment. This fear often led her to make impulsive phone calls, send desperate texts, or engage in self-destructive behaviors to regain a sense of control. Exhausted by the emotional roller coaster, Sarah sought therapy specializing in BPD.

Therapy and Beyond: Tools for Change

Angel's therapist helped her understand the roots of her fear of abandonment and its impact on her life. Here are some key strategies that helped Angel overcome it:

- **Cognitive Behavioral Therapy (CBT):** CBT helped Angel identify and challenge her negative thought patterns surrounding abandonment. She learned to re-frame situations and recognize that perceived slights weren't always a sign of someone leaving.
- **Dialectical Behavior Therapy (DBT):** DBT equipped Angel with valuable skills to manage her emotions. Mindfulness practices helped her recover from intense feelings and respond rather than react. Distress tolerance skills helped her navigate emotional distress without resorting to self destructive behaviors.
- **Building Healthy Relationships:** Angel's therapist helped her set healthy boundaries in her relationships and communicate her needs assertively. This reduced clingy behavior and fostered trust and mutual respect.
- **Self-Compassion and Self-Care:** Angel learned to treat herself with kindness and understanding. They practiced self-care activities like journaling, meditation, and spend-

ing time with supportive loved ones, which nurtured her self-worth and reduced the need for external validation.

The Road to Recovery

It wasn't an easy journey. There were setbacks and moments of intense fear. However, through consistent therapy, self-awareness, and dedication to practicing new skills, Angel gradually began to see a change. She started developing healthier relationships, her emotions became more manageable, and the constant anxiety around abandonment subsided.

Key Takeaways from Angel's Story
Angel's story offers valuable insights to readers:

- *The fear of abandonment can be overcome with the right approach.*
- *Therapy provides a safe space to understand the roots of your fear and learn coping mechanisms.*
- *Developing self-compassion and practicing self-care are crucial for building emotional resilience.*
- *Change takes time and consistent effort. Celebrate small victories, and don't be discouraged by setbacks.*

Remember, you are not alone. Many individuals with BPD have successfully overcome the fear of abandonment. By incorporating the tools and strategies discussed in this chapter, you, too, can build healthy relationships, manage your emotions, and create a fulfilling life.

Case Study 5:

The Ripple Effect of Reckless Spending; Story of Sarah Jr

Brief details of Sarah Jr;

This case study explores the societal impact of impulsivity in BPD through the experiences of Sarah, a young adult grappling with the consequences of her reckless spending habits. Sarah's story illustrates how impulsivity associated with BPD can lead to financial strain, disrupt social connections, and create a burden on both the individual and society.

Sarah's Story

Sarah, a 23-year-old college graduate, was diagnosed with BPD shortly after entering the workforce. One of her primary struggles was impulsivity, particularly around spending. Fueled by intense emotions and a desire for instant gratification, Sarah often made impulsive purchases, disregarding consequences or her limited budget. She'd buy designer clothing on a whim, rack up credit card debt on dining experiences and entertainment, and fall prey to targeted online advertisements.

The Financial Fallout

Sarah's impulsive spending quickly spiraled into significant debt. Credit card bills piled up, and minimum payments became a challenge. She began neglecting essential bills like rent and utilities, jeopardizing her housing situation. The constant financial pressure fueled anxiety and shame, worsening her emotional state and triggering further impulsive spending as a coping mechanism.

Impact on Social Relationships

Sarah's financial struggles strained her relationships with family and friends. Concerned about her mounting debt, her parents offered financial assistance with strict conditions. However, Sarah's impulsivity often led to breaking these conditions, further eroding trust. Friendships also suffered as Sarah could no longer afford to participate in social activities or offer reciprocal support. The shame associated with her financial situation led to social isolation, deepening her sense of loneliness and despair.

Societal Costs

Sarah's story highlights the societal impact of impulsivity in BPD. Her financial difficulties placed a burden on the public healthcare system. Mounting debt and missed payments affected credit card companies, potentially impacting interest rates for others. Her eviction created a vacancy in the rental market, contributing to the housing shortage in some areas.

A Missed Contribution

Sarah, a bright college graduate, struggled to find stable employment due to her emotional dysregulation and the stress of her financial situation. Her potential contribution to the workforce remained unrealized, impacting the overall economic productivity.

A Path Towards Hope

Sarah eventually sought professional help. Therapy sessions focused on managing her impulsivity and developing healthier coping mechanisms for emotional distress. She learned budgeting skills and explored debt management options. Reconciling with her parents involved open communication and rebuilding trust. It was a long and challenging process, but Sarah gradually gained control of her finances and reconnected with loved ones.

Takeaway from Sarah's Story

Sarah's story serves as a stark reminder of the societal impact of impulsivity in BPD. It highlights the importance of early intervention and treatment to equip individuals with the skills to manage their impulsivity and participate productively in society. Increased public awareness and support systems can help bridge the gap between struggling individuals and the resources they need to thrive.

Case Study 6;

The Cycle of Substance Abuse: Case Study of David

Introduction

This case study explores the societal impact of impulsivity in BPD through the experiences of David, an individual battling substance abuse. David's story illustrates how impulsivity associated with BPD can lead to a cycle of substance abuse, job losses, and reliance on public resources, straining the economic and social fabric.

David's Journey

David, a 42-year-old man, has lived with BPD since his teenage years. One of his most prominent struggles was impulsivity, often manifested in risky behaviors like substance abuse. Driven by intense emotions and difficulty regulating his moods, David turned to alcohol and drugs as a coping mechanism. These substances initially offered a temporary escape from emotional pain but ultimately worsened his mental health and overall functioning.

Health Deterioration and Job Losses

David's substance abuse habits had a significant impact on his health. His physical health suffered due to neglect and the adverse effects of drugs and alcohol. His mental health also deteriorated, with episodes of depression and anxiety becoming more frequent. These health issues impacted his ability to maintain stable employment. Absenteeism decreased productivity, and erratic behavior due to his BPD symptoms often led to job losses.

Reliance on Public Resources

David's frequent unemployment made it difficult to afford health insurance and proper medical care. He relied heavily on public healthcare clinics and emergency room visits for treatment of his health problems stemming from substance abuse. Additionally, his inability to maintain consistent employment made him financially dependent on social assistance programs.

Takeaway from David's Story

David's story shows how minor errors in adulthood complicate everyday life and ultimately ruin life, and here, only strong willpower can help you escape such a mess.

Case Study 7:

Scars on Society: Self-Harm in Public and the Ripple Effect. Story of Mark.

Introduction

Mark, a 32-year-old struggling with Borderline Personality Disorder (BPD), finds himself caught in a storm of intense emotions. The overwhelming nature of these emotions, coupled with difficulty regulating them, leads him to engage in self-harm – a hallmark symptom of BPD. This case study explores the aftermath of Mark's self-harm episode in a public space, highlighting the societal impact it creates, from emotional distress to the strain on emergency services and public safety.

The Trigger and the Act

Mark's BPD manifests in intense fear of abandonment and a distorted self-image. He recently ended a tumultuous relationship, leaving him feeling isolated and worthless. The emotional pain feels unbearable, and the familiar urge to self-harm arises. He finds himself in a crowded park, the noise and activity creating a sense of detachment. In a public restroom stall, he uses a sharp object to inflict self-harm, seeking a release from the emotional turmoil.

A Cascade of Consequences

The self-harm episode leaves Mark with physical injuries and a more profound sense of shame and isolation. However, the repercussions extend far beyond him.

- **Distressed Bystanders:** A young couple exiting the restroom stumbles upon Mark, witnessing the aftermath of his self-harm. They are shocked and unsure how to react. The graphic image leaves them emotionally shaken, impacting their day and potentially triggering their anxieties.
- **Emergency Services Intervention:** The couple alerts park security, who call emergency medical services. Ambulance sirens pierce the air, drawing attention and causing a commotion. Paramedics arrive, stabilizing Mark and transporting him to the nearest emergency room.

The Burden on Resources

Mark's self-harm episode strains valuable societal resources:

- **Emergency Medical Services:** Ambulances and emergency medical personnel are stretched thin, responding to numerous calls daily. Mark's case diverts resources from potential emergencies, highlighting the pressure on healthcare systems.
- **Hospital Resources:** Mark occupies a bed in the emergency room and requires medical attention from already overworked doctors and nurses. This adds to the strain on hospital capacity and delays treatment for other patients.
- **Mental Health Professionals:** Ideally, after the initial medical assessment, Mark would benefit from a mental health professional evaluation. However, limited access to mental health services can create delays in receiving crucial support.

Public Safety Concerns

Self-harm in a public space can also pose public safety risks:

- **Unpredictable Behavior:** The emotional distress leading to self-harm can be unpredictable. In some cases, individuals might engage in self-harm with suicidal intent, creating a potential safety hazard for themselves and others.
- **Public Panic:** The sight of self-harm can be disturbing, leading to panic or anxiety among bystanders. This can create a chaotic situation requiring intervention from law enforcement or security personnel.

Breaking the Cycle

Mark's story underscores the societal impact of self-harm associated with BPD. Here's how we can work towards mitigating these consequences:

- **Increased Awareness:** Educating the public about BPD and self-harm can help bystanders understand the situation better and respond with compassion rather than fear. Educational campaigns can also encourage people struggling with self-harm to seek help.
- **Improved Access to Mental Healthcare:** Ensuring more comprehensive access to affordable, high-quality mental healthcare services is crucial. Early intervention and practical treatment approaches like Dialectical Behavior Therapy (DBT) can equip individuals with BPD with healthier coping mechanisms to manage emotional distress, reducing the likelihood of self-harm.
- **Crisis Intervention Training:** Training public safety per-

sonnel and park security on responding effectively to self-harm incidents can minimize public panic and ensure the safety of individuals and bystanders. Additionally, training can connect individuals with appropriate mental health resources.

Takeaway from Mark's Story: A Society Built on Understanding
Mark's story serves as a stark reminder of the societal impact of self-harm in BPD. By fostering a more understanding society, improving access to mental healthcare, and implementing crisis intervention training, we can create a support system that helps individuals struggling with BPD manage their emotions in healthier ways. This benefits them by reducing the strain on emergency services and promoting public safety.

Note: This case study is fictional and does not represent any specific individual. However, it reflects the real-life challenges faced by many individuals with BPD and highlights the societal impact of their struggles.

Case Study -8;

A Case of Emily and her Disturbed Self-Image due to Borderline Personality Disorder.

Introduction: Borderline Personality Disorder (BPD) is a complex mental health condition characterized by intense emotions, unstable relationships, and a distorted self-image. This chapter delves into the experience of a disturbed self-image in BPD, using a fictionalized case study interwoven with real-world research findings to illustrate the challenges faced by individuals in the United States.

Meet Emily: A Fragile Identity, A Case of Disturbed Self-Image

Emily, a 25-year-old aspiring artist living in Los Angeles, embodies the struggle with a disturbed self-image in BPD. Her artistic talent is undeniable, yet her perception of herself constantly shifts.

Once day, she feels radiant and confident, convinced her artwork is on the verge of recognition. The next day, a harsh inner critic takes over, dismantling her creations and leaving her feeling like a fraud. This constant fluctuation in self-perception reflects the core challenge of a disturbed self-image in BPD.

Understanding the Disturbed Self-Image in BPD

Imagine looking in the mirror, but the reflection keeps changing. That's the essence of a disturbed self-image in BPD. Here's a breakdown of this core feature:

- **Fragmented Identity:** Individuals with BPD often struggle to develop a stable sense of self. Their core values, beliefs, and goals are constantly in flux, leaving them feeling like a collection of disconnected parts rather than a whole person.
- **Fear of Abandonment:** The intense fear of abandonment central to BPD fuels a distorted self-image. Emily might believe she needs to be perfect or constantly please others to avoid rejection, leading to a chameleon-like adaptation to situations.
- **Emotional Dysregulation:** The inability to regulate emotions significantly impacts self-perception. An unfavorable evaluation from a friend can trigger feelings of worthlessness and shatter Emily's fragile sense of self.

The Interactive Experience: Stepping into Emily's Shoes

Imagine scrolling through Emily's social media feed. One day, it's filled with vibrant photos of her artwork and captions expressing immense pride. The next day, the feed lacks new posts, and the profile picture is replaced with a generic image. This reflects the fluctuating self-image and the fear of judgment that might make Emily withdraw when feeling insecure.

Research Spotlight: The Facts Behind the Experience

Research in the United States supports the experience of a disturbed self-image in BPD. Here are some key findings:

- A study published in the Journal of Personality Disorders found that individuals with BPD reported significantly lower self-esteem and a more negative self-image compared to control groups.

- Researchers at the University of Washington found that people with BPD exhibited a heightened sensitivity to social feedback, particularly negative evaluations, further reinforcing the fear of abandonment and leading to a more critical self-perception.

The Societal Impact: Beyond the Individual

Emily's struggle with self-image spills over into her social life:

- **Unstable Relationships:** Difficulty maintaining stable relationships is a hallmark of BPD. Emily's constant need for validation can be overwhelming for friends and partners, leading to conflict and potential abandonment.
- **Career Challenges:** The erratic self-perception can hinder professional pursuits. Emily might struggle to commit to a specific artistic style or doubt her ability to succeed in the competitive art world.
- **Increased Vulnerability:** A distorted self-image can make individuals with BPD more susceptible to manipulation or exploitation, posing a significant social risk.

Interactive Activity: Breaking the Mirror: Rebuilding Self-Image

Imagine a support group session for individuals with BPD. Here, Emily can connect with others who understand her struggle. The group facilitator guides them through exercises like:

- **Identifying Core Values:** By exploring what truly matters to them, individuals like Emily can build a more stable sense of self beyond external validation.
- **Challenging Negative Self-Talk:** Identifying and replacing negative self-criticism with more compassionate self-talk can empower Emily to view herself with kindness and acceptance.
- **Celebrating Achievements:** Recognizing and celebrating accomplishments, both big and small, can help rebuild self-confidence and foster a more positive self-image.

The Road to Recovery: Treatment Options in the USA

Fortunately, BPD is treatable. Here are some evidence-based therapies available in the United States that can help individuals like Emily:

- **Dialectical Behavior Therapy (DBT):** DBT equips individuals with skills to manage emotions, regulate distress tolerance, improve communication, and build healthier interpersonal relationships.
- **Cognitive Behavioral Therapy (CBT) helps identify and challenge negative thought patterns that contribute** to a distorted self-image and develop more adaptive coping mechanisms.
- **Schema Therapy:** This therapy

Takeaway from Emily's Story

Emily's story shows how minor errors in adulthood ruin life, and only strong willpower can help you escape such a mess. This reflects the fluctuating self-image and the fear of judgment that might make Emily withdraw when feeling insecure.

Note: This case study is fictional and does not represent any specific individual. However, it reflects the real-life challenges faced by many individuals with BPD and highlights the societal impact of their struggles.

16

Handling BPD with the help of Dialectical Behavior Therapy (DBT)

Unveiling the Power of DBT, A Guide to Emotional Mastery

Dialectical Behavior Therapy (DBT) has emerged as a beacon of hope for individuals struggling with Borderline Personality Disorder (BPD). Imagine a person who was always earlier consumed by overwhelming emotions is now equipped to use these powerful tools to navigate life's challenges. This guide delves into DBT, exploring how it empowers individuals to cultivate emotional regulation, healthy relationships, and a fulfilling life.

Understanding the Landscape: BPD and the Need for Dialectical Behavior Therapy (DBT)

Borderline Personality Disorder presents a complex set of challenges. People with BPD often experience intense emotions that can feel overwhelming and lead to impulsive behaviors or difficulty maintaining healthy relationships. Traditional therapy approaches sometimes fall short of addressing these complexities.DBT, developed by Marsha Linehan, explicitly targets BPD's core difficulties, offering a structured and skills-based approach to emotional mastery.

The DBT Toolbox: Equipping You for Success

Dialectical Behavior Therapy(DBT) equips individuals with four core sets of skills, forming a comprehensive toolbox for emotional well-being. **These Four Core Skills are;**

1. **Mindfulness:** This skill focuses on living in the present moment, objectively observing thoughts and emotions without judgment. Imagine being caught in a storm of emotions. Mindfulness allows you to step back, acknowledge the intensity, and avoid being swept away.
2. **Emotional Regulation:** DBT teaches techniques to manage overwhelming emotions effectively. Just as you wouldn't fight a fire with gasoline, DBT equips you with healthy coping mechanisms to navigate emotional turmoil. This could involve relaxation techniques like deep breathing, distraction strategies, or identifying the

underlying needs driving your emotions.

3. **Distress Tolerance:** Life throws curve balls. DBT teaches skills to tolerate distress without resorting to self-destructive behaviors. It's like learning to ride the waves of emotions rather than being capsized. Techniques include radical acceptance, where you acknowledge the difficulty of a situation without judgment, and crisis survival skills to manage intense moments effectively.

4. **Interpersonal Effectiveness:** Healthy relationships are crucial for well-being. DBT equips individuals with communication skills to express needs assertively, set boundaries, and navigate conflict productively. Imagine being able to have honest conversations without resorting to manipulation or withdrawal. DBT empowers you to build and maintain fulfilling relationships.

Remember that Dialectical Behavior Therapy (DBT) isn't just about theory; it's about equipping you with practical skills to navigate life's challenges. Imagine feeling overwhelmed by anxiety, yet instead of being swept away, you have a toolbox of techniques to manage it effectively. These techniques can be interactive exercises designed to put DBT principles into action.

These Tool Box Techniques are:

1. Cultivating Calm by using Mindfulness Exercises every day:

Mindfulness is the foundation of DBT. It's about observing your thoughts and emotions without judgment, allowing you to respond rather than react. Here's an interactive exercise to get you started:

- **Finding Your Quiet Space:** Locate a comfortable, quiet area in your home or workplace. This could be a designated meditation space, a cozy corner, or even a park bench surrounded by nature.
- **Settling In:** Sit comfortably with your back straight but not rigid. You can sit on a chair with your feet flat on the floor or cross-legged on a cushion. Close your eyes gently or soften your gaze if that feels more comfortable.
- **The Breath Anchor:** Focus on your breath. Feel the rise and fall of your chest with each inhalation and exhalation. If your mind wanders perfectly normal, gently bring it back to your breath without judgment.
- **Engaging Your Senses:** Incorporate your senses to expand your mindfulness practice. Notice the sounds around you, the temperature of the air on your skin, or the subtle sensations in your body.
- **Practice Makes Progress:** Aim for 5-10 minutes of daily mindfulness practice. Consistency is key. Even short bursts throughout the day can significantly enhance your emotional awareness.
- **Decoding Your Triggers: Identifying the Emotional**

Storms: Triggers are situations or events that evoke intense emotions. Recognizing your triggers is crucial for applying DBT skills effectively. Here's an interactive exercise to identify yours:

- **Emotional Weather Report:** Reflect on the past week. When did you experience intense emotions like anger, sadness, or anxiety? Jot down these situations in a journal.
- **Digging Deeper:** Analyze the common threads in these situations. What specific events or interactions triggered these emotions?
- **Early Warning Signs:** Pay attention to your body's signals. Does your heart race? Do your palms sweat? Identifying these physical cues can help you recognize a trigger before it escalates.
- **Creating a Trigger List:** Develop a running list of your triggers. This will be a valuable reference point when practicing other DBT skills.

2. Building Your Resilience: Distress Tolerance Toolbox

Life throws curveballs, and distress is inevitable. DBT teaches distress tolerance skills to navigate complex emotions without resorting to self-destructive behaviors. **Let's create a personalized "crisis survival kit":**

- **Calming Toolkit:** List activities that bring you a sense of Calm. This could include listening to soothing music, taking a nature walk, reading a favorite book, or practicing deep breathing exercises.

- **Soothing Sensations:** Identify sensory experiences that calm you. These could include taking a warm bath, indulging in a cup of herbal tea, or wrapping yourself in a soft blanket.
- **Reaching Out:** Compile a list of trusted individuals you can contact during distress. This could be a friend, family member, therapist, or support group hotlink.
- **Crisis Survival Plan:** Develop a step-by-step plan for your actions when triggered. This might involve using your calming toolkit, reaching for support, or engaging in a safe, self-soothing activity.

Remember: This is your toolbox. Customize it with strategies that work best for you. Practice using these tools regularly so they become second nature when faced with distress.

3. Beyond the Exercises: Deepening Your DBT Journey

These interactive exercises are a springboard for your DBT journey. Remember, DBT is a comprehensive approach, and these practices are most effective when combined with individual therapy and group skills training. Here are some additional tips to support your learning:

- **Embrace Self-Compassion:** Be kind to yourself. Learning new skills takes time and practice. Don't get discouraged by setbacks. Acknowledge your progress and celebrate your victories, no matter how small.
- **Self-Care is Essential:** Prioritize activities that nourish

your mind, body, and spirit. This might include getting enough sleep, eating healthy meals, exercising regularly, and engaging in hobbies you enjoy.

· **Explore Additional Resources:** Numerous resources are available to deepen your understanding of DBT. Consider books on DBT skills, online courses, or support groups specifically for individuals practicing.

Challenges in using the Dialectical Behavior Therapy (DBT) technique by Self and suggested Solutions.

There are specific Challenges in using DBT technique by one-self. At this moment, I mention these and provide suggestive solutions to overcome them. These are:

Embracing the Learning Curve;

1. **Motivation and Commitment:** DBT therapy requires dedication and consistent effort. Attending sessions, practicing, and integrating skills into daily life can sometimes feel overwhelming.

· **Solution:** Break down goals into smaller, achievable steps. Celebrate each success, no matter how small. Utilize reminders and reward systems to stay on track. Consider joining a DBT support group for additional encouragement and accountability.

2. **Facing Uncomfortable Emotions:** DBT encourages the exploration of painful emotions. This can be difficult and trigger avoidance behaviors.

- **Solution:** Acknowledge that experiencing these emotions is a necessary part of healing—practice mindfulness techniques like deep breathing and visualization to manage intense feelings without impulsivity. Remember, your therapist guides and supports you through this process.

3. **Feeling Invalidated:** It's possible to feel misunderstood by loved ones while practicing new skills. This can be discouraging.

- **Solution:** Communicate openly with your support system about your DBT journey. Explain how you're working on managing emotions and coping with difficult situations. Provide resources like educational materials about DBT to help them understand your process.

4. **Feeling Stuck:** Progress can feel slow at times. This can lead to frustration and a desire to give up.

- **Solution:** Track your progress through journals, workbooks, or progress charts. Celebrate even minor improvements. Remember, change takes time and consistent effort. Discuss any roadblocks with your therapist and explore alternative strategies.

5. Interpersonal Conflict: DBT skills like assertive communication are often new, and practicing them can initially lead to conflict.

. **Solution:** Seek support from your therapist to navigate these conflicts effectively. Utilize role-playing exercises to practice using communication skills before real-life situations arise. Remember, communication is a two-way street, and your loved ones may also need some time to adjust to the changes in your communication style.

The Power of Self-Compassion: Fueling Your DBT Journey

I want to elaborate more on the power of self-compassion. DBT isn't just about mastering skills; it's about cultivating a kinder and more understanding relationship with yourself. Self-compassion is vital for navigating challenges and staying motivated throughout your DBT journey. Here's how to nurture it:

- **Challenge Self-Criticism:** Notice your inner critic and replace harsh judgment with self-affirmations. Acknowledge your progress and celebrate your accomplishments.
- **Embrace Imperfection:** Recognize that setbacks and mistakes are part of learning. Don't let them define you. Learn from them and move forward with self-compassion.
- **Practice Mindfulness of Self:** Take time for introspection. Reflect on your needs and emotions without judgment. Treat yourself with the same kindness you would offer a close friend.

Self-Care: The Foundation for Well-being

Self-care isn't a luxury; it's a necessity. Just like a car needs regular maintenance to run smoothly, you must prioritize activities that nourish your mind, body, and spirit.

- **Prioritize Sleep:** Aim for 7-8 hours of quality sleep each night. Develop a relaxing bedtime routine and establish a consistent sleep schedule.
- **Nourish Your Body:** Eat healthy, balanced meals that fuel your energy and well-being. Stay hydrated throughout the day.
- **Move Your Body:** Physical activity is a natural mood booster. Find an exercise routine you enjoy brisk walking, dancing, or team sports.
- **Mind-Body Practices:** Activities like yoga, meditation,

or deep breathing exercises can promote relaxation and emotional regulation. Explore different techniques to find what works best for you.

- **Engage in Activities You Enjoy:** Make time for hobbies and activities that bring you joy. This could be reading, spending time in nature, listening to music, or socializing with loved ones.

Remember, Self-care is a continuous journey, not a one-time event. Listen to your body's needs and adjust your self-care routines accordingly.

17

Checklist for BPD Persons: 10 Steps for Successful & Happy Living

"What I love about therapy is that they'll tell you what your blind spots are. Although uncomfortable and painful, it gives you something to work with." — Pink.

****

" THE ONLY WAY TO GET THE BEST OF AN ARGUMENT IS TO AVOID IT"- Dale Carnegie.

****

Here, I have compiled a checklist for people with Borderline Personality Disorder (BPD) to consider adopting in their life for a happier and more fulfilling life:

1. **Educate Yourself:** Learn about BPD and its symptoms and strategies for managing the Disorder. Understanding the conditions can help individuals gain insight into their experiences and develop effective coping mechanisms.

2. **Practice Mindfulness**: Mindfulness techniques can help individuals with BPD ground themselves in the present moment, reducing emotional reactivity and promoting emotional regulation. Examples include deep breathing exercises, body scans, and meditation.

3. **Develop Interpersonal Effectiveness Skills:** Effective communication and boundary-setting skills can significantly improve relationships. These skills involve assertively expressing needs and desires, listening actively, and negotiating conflicts healthily.

4. **Build a Support Network**: Surround yourself with supportive and understanding individuals who can offer emotional support and encouragement. **Friends and family are the most important supporters; support groups or online communities can help**.

5. **Consider Medication**: Consult with a psychiatrist to decide

the most suitable medication options that can help manage symptoms like depression, anxiety, or mood swings. Medication works as a valuable tool when used in conjunction with therapy.

6. Engage in Self-Care: Prioritize activities that promote self-care and well-being. These include hobbies, relaxation techniques, regular exercise, a healthy diet, and ensuring adequate sleep.

7. Develop Emotional Regulation Skills: Learn practical strategies to manage intense emotions. This can involve identifying triggers, using grounding techniques, engaging in self-soothing activities, and utilizing distraction techniques when needed. AVOID getting into arguments and passing negative comments on others to avoid getting hurt by others' reactions. This will help maintain one's emotional well-being.

8. Create a Safety Plan: Develop a safety plan in collaboration with your therapist to manage crises and prevent self-harm or suicidal thoughts. This plan can include emergency contacts, coping strategies, and steps to take during a crisis.

9. Seek Professional Help: Find a licensed mental health professional, psychologist, or psychiatrist specializing in treating BPD. They can provide guidance, support, and evidence-based therapies. **The toolkit of Dialectical Behavior Therapy (DBT), as discussed in Chapter 19, will significantly help bring balance to your life. For this purpose, a person affected by BPD or his family members should read Chapter 19, understand it well, and implement it in their life as a tool for self-control. I**

am confident that this act will significantly help you maintain emotional control.

10. Setting Realistic Goals In Daily Routine: Break down more significant milestones into smaller ones, making them achievable. Celebrate each milestone along the way, as this can boost motivation and self-confidence. Prioritizing the jobs based on priorities /urgency will also greatly help.

Remember, recovery is not straightforward; it's a unique journey that varies from person to person, and progress often occurs in small, incremental steps. Hence, the patient's role becomes crucial, and being patient and kind to yourself throughout the process is essential. Additionally, a regular reassessment of progress and adjusting the checklist based on individual needs and progress are also necessary.

Some Additional Related Conditions to be Monitored and Noticed

BPD can be difficult to diagnose for a successful treatment and addressing any other conditions a person might have. It is observed that many people having BPD also experience the following additional conditions:

- Anxiety Disorders

- Post-traumatic Stress Disorder
- Bipolar Disorder
- Depression
- Eating Disorders (notably bulimia nervosa)
- Substance Use Disorders / Dual Diagnosis

18

YOGA; 5 Yoga Exercises for Overall Well-being

Yoga can be a great tool for promoting peace, focus, and overall well-being. However, it's important to note that yoga should be used as a complementary practice alongside professional treatment for borderline personality disorder.It's always a good idea to consult a certified yoga instructor or therapist who can guide you through these exercises and tailor them to your needs.

Here are a few yoga exercises that may help;

:1. Deep Breathing (Pranayama):

Start by sitting comfortably with your eyes closed. Take slow, deep breaths, focusing on the sensation of the breath entering and leaving your body. This exercise can help calm the mind and reduce anxiety.

2. Tree Pose (Vrikshasana):

Stand tall with your feet hip-width apart. Shift your weight onto one leg and place the sole of your other foot on your inner thigh or calf. Find your balance and bring your hands to your heart center. This pose helps improve focus and stability.

3. Warrior II (Virabhadrasana II):

Stand with your feet wide apart, turn your right foot out, and bend your right knee. Extend your arms out to the sides, parallel to the floor. Gaze over your right hand. This pose can help cultivate strength, confidence, and focus.

4. Child's Pose (Balasana):

Start kneeling on the floor, then sit back on your heels. Lower your torso between your thighs and extend your arms forward. Rest your forehead on the mat or a block. This pose promotes relaxation and helps release tension in the body.

5. Legs-Up-The-Wall Pose (Viparita Karani):

Sit sideways next to a wall and swing your legs onto the wall as you lie back on the floor. Extend your arms out to the sides, palms facing up. This gentle inversion pose can help calm the nervous system and reduce stress.

While yoga has excellent benefits, we should avoid doing it alone at home without a trained supervisor. It's always a good idea to consult a certified yoga instructor or therapist who can guide you through these exercises and tailor them to your needs.

Also, always listen to your body and practice within your limits.

Beyond Yoga: Some More Simple Practices/Techniques

While yoga has excellent benefits, some simple techniques can easily be incorporated into our daily lives. These are mentioned as follows;

Meditation –

It is the traditional way of achieving mental peace and calm. It is also beneficial when compared to other therapeutic techniques. Find a comfortable place and try to quiet the mind. Get started with basic meditation, like focusing on breathing and feeling the body, and then explore the different meditation techniques, like spiritual meditation, which includes chanting prayer; mindfulness meditation, which includes learning to rest through combining concentration with awareness; movement meditation, etc.

Deep Breathing

Focusing on the sound and rhythm of breath, especially when people are upset, can have a soothing effect and help them stay grounded in the current, using breathing exercises throughout the day.

Music therapy–

It is a new branch of complementary medicine. A particular type of music can make us happy, sad, energetic, or relaxed. It has a unique impact on a person's mindset. Due to its innumerable impacts, music has been recognized as a helpful treatment for people with personality disorders.

Observing Thoughts –

The mindfulness exercise of observing our thoughts might help decrease the symptoms of personality disorders. Instead of reacting against the voice, sitting back and "observing" thoughts without involvement can help achieve peace. It can be the best exercise to find the solutions to some hidden questions; in this way, the thoughts become less stressful. However, it is not as easy as it appears, but observing the thoughts can make it easy and be the best way to understand the thoughts rendering in mind.

Art Therapy –

Like music therapy, it is a branch of complementary medicine and has been proven very effective in treating BPD. A therapist can help explain the figures to learn more about oneself.

According to a recent study by Harvard Medical School published in 2009,

The technique of Sudarshan Kriya yoga (a type of yoga) was found to be most effective in reducing the symptoms of anxiety and depression. The method is inexpensive and risk–free and positively connects our mind and body. There are various yoga techniques, but Breathing deeply is one of the simplest relaxation methods. It can positively affect our immune system and increase our awareness of the body, irregular moods, and unproductive behavior patterns.

19

Mindfulness Techniques for Self Help

"The experience I have had is that once you start talking about [experiencing a mental health struggle], you realize that you're part of quite a big club." — Prince Harry

Knowing about Mindfulness in Borderline personality Disorder

Many biopsychosocial models of borderline personality disorder (BPD) center on emotion dysregulation, which is frequently addressed in the psycho-social therapies that are linked to the management of the disorder. For those with BPD diagnoses, several different specialized psychotherapies are believed to be helpful, but it's uncertain if they have similar changing mechanisms. Many psychotherapies include mindfulness as a component. However, its usefulness in the treatment of

137

borderline personality disorder (BPD) is still unclear.

The purpose of the concern study is to examine the effect of mindfulness practices in the management of borderline personality disorder incorporating medication. A sample of 50 borderline-old patients [clinical diagnosis having the borderline personality disorder (BPD) severity score of more than 20 points on [BPDSI] were purposively selected for the study. The patients were given regular medication incorporating the mindfulness exercises. After six months, the symptoms were checked through a mental health checklist. Professionals administered a mental health checklist before and after integrating mindfulness with the medication.

The study revealed that the most commonly improved symptoms were adequate instability, inappropriate anger, and feelings of emptiness. Kundalini Yoga (64%) and Sudarshan Kriya (58%) were the most effective mindfulness practices in decreasing the symptoms of BPD. The study revealed that mindfulness practices have a vast impact on reducing the symptoms of BPD while incorporating medications. Several mindfulness techniques are pretty successful in symptom reduction. Professionals are including mindfulness meditation training in their treatment regimens since it promotes physical and mental stability. Training in mindfulness/meditation is a requirement of social work practice nowadays. It could be valuable in social work education to explore their thinking and to evaluate their personality traits and behavioral patterns. These practices naturally enhance creativity and imagination.

In addition to yoga exercises, Mindfulness Techniques can be instrumental in calming oneself and being in control. These FEW simple yet effective techniques are explained with live examples:

1. Mindful Breathing Techniques:

- Find a quiet and comfortable place to sit or lie down.
- Close your eyes and bring your attention to your breath.
- Notice the sensation of the breath as it enters and leaves your body.
- Focus on the rise and fall of your abdomen or the feeling of air passing through your nostrils.
- If your mind wanders, gently bring your attention back to your breath without judgment.
- Practice this for a few minutes or as long as you'd like.

Example:

Imagine you're sitting outside on a sunny day. Close your eyes and take a few deep breaths. As you inhale, notice the warmth of the sun on your skin. As you exhale, feel the gentle breeze against your face. Allow yourself to fully experience the present moment, letting go of any thoughts or worries.

2. Body Scan Technique:

- Find a comfortable position, either sitting or lying down.
- Close your eyes and bring your attention to your body.
- Starting from the top of your head, slowly scan down

through your body, noticing any sensations or areas of tension.

- As you encounter areas of tension, consciously relax those muscles and release any tightness.

- Continue scanning down through your body, bringing awareness to each part.

- Notice any thoughts or emotions that arise without judgment, then gently bring your attention back to the body.

Example:

Lie down on a yoga mat or comfortable surface. Close your eyes and begin to scan your body from head to toe. As you move your attention down, notice any areas of tightness or discomfort. Take a deep breath, and as you exhale, consciously release any tension in those areas. Continue the body scan, bringing awareness to each part of your body and allowing yourself to relax and let go entirely.

3. Mindful Walking Technique:

- Find a quiet and safe space to walk indoors or outdoors.

- Begin by standing still and bringing your attention to your body and breath.

- Slowly start walking, paying attention to the sensation of your feet touching the ground.

- Notice the movement of your legs, the swinging of your arms, and the overall sensation of walking.

- If your mind starts to wander, gently bring your attention back to the physical sensations of walking.

- Engage all your senses by noticing the sights, sounds, and smells around you as you walk.

Example:

Take a leisurely walk in a nearby park or garden. As you walk, focus on the feeling of your feet touching the ground. Notice the texture of the path beneath your feet, the rhythm of your steps, and the movement of your body. Observe the colors and shapes of the flowers, the sounds of birds chirping, and the scent of nature. Allow yourself to fully immerse in the present moment and appreciate the beauty around you.

20

Some Suggestion For Treatment And Research Advancements Association For Personality Disorder

Here is a list of various institutions that can help you in the treatment of personality disorder;

National Nonprofit Organization;
www.tara4bpd.org

A national nonprofit organization advocates for individuals with BPD and their families. It sponsors workshops and seminars, operates a national resource and referral center, and articulates BPD issues to congressional legislators.

Treatment Centers

A. MCLEAN HOSPITAL
115 Mill Street
Belmont, MA 02478
877-372-3068

B. NEW YORK-PRESBYTERIAN WESTCHESTER BEHAVIORAL
HEALTH CENTER
21 Bloomingdale Road
White Plains, NY 10605
888-694-5700
914-682-9100

C. AUSTEN RIGGS CENTER
25 Main Street
Stockbridge, MA 01262
austenriggs.org/borderline-personality-disorder-treatment
800-51-RIGGS.

D. SILVER HILL HOSPITAL
208 Valley Road
New Canaan, CT 06840
866-542-4455
www.SilverHillHospital.org

21

Websites(Suggested) For More Learning Information on Borderline Personality Disorder

Websites For Learning More about Borderline Personality Disorder;

Mental Health Organizations:

- **National Alliance on Mental Illness (NAMI):** https://www.nami.org/ (1-800-950-NAMI (6264)) - Provides information, support groups, and advocacy for individuals with mental illness and their families.
- **National Institute of Mental Health (NIMH):** https://www.nimh.nih.gov/ - Offers resources and information on BPD, including treatment options and clinical trials.
- **Mental Health.gov:** https://www.samhsa.gov/mental-health -A U.S. government t website providing information and resources on various mental health conditions.

- **Mayo Clinic Information can be found at https://**mayoclinic.com/health/borderline-personality-disorder/ DS00442. It provides general information and answers to questions.
- **National Education Alliance For Borderline Personality Disorder (NEA-BPD);** WWW.borderlinepersonalitydisorder.com- Support and education for patients, relatives, and professionals.
- **American Psychiatric Association (APA):** Briefly mention that the APA publishes the DSM-5, the standard reference for diagnosing mental disorders, including BPD.
- **National Alliance on Mental Illness (NAMI):** You can highlight NAMI as a valuable resource for individuals with BPD and their families, offering support groups and educational materials.
- **National Institute Of Mental Health;** www.nimh.nih.gov/health/ publications/borderline-personality disorder. More information can be seen.

Some Other Sites;
BORDERLINE PERSONALITY DISORDER DEMYSTIFIED
www.bpddemystified.com
This is a general site animated by Robert O. Friedel, MD, a leading psychiatrist and author of Borderline Personality Disorder Demystified.

BORDERLINE PERSONALITY DISORDER RESOURCE CENTER
bpdresourcecenter@nyp.org 888-694-2273
Provides educational materials and treatment resources.

BPD CENTRAL;WEBSITES(SUGGESTED) FOR MORE LEARNING INFORMATION ON...

WWW.bpdcentral.com

It is one of the oldest sites, with many suggested books and articles.

BPD RECOVERY

WWW.bpdrecovery.com

A site for individuals recovering from BPD, emphasizing cognitive-behavioral treatment.

FACING THE FACTS

WWW.bpdfamily.com

It is one of the largest sites that provides information and support for families.

22

Knowing and Building Your Support Network

Our journey towards overcoming abandonment anxiety and fostering secure relationships is a continuous process. This book equips you with valuable tools and strategies; additional resources can provide further support and guidance. Here's a comprehensive list to empower you on your path:

Mental Health Organizations:

- **National Alliance on Mental Illness (NAMI):** https://www.nami.org/ (1–800–950–NAMI (6264)) – Provides information, support groups, and advocacy for individuals with mental illness and their families.
- **National Institute of Mental Health (NIMH):** https://www.nimh.nih.gov/ – Offers resources and information on BPD, including treatment options and clinical trials.
- **MentalHealth.gov:** https://www.samhsa.gov/mental-health – A U.S. government website providing information and resources on various mental health conditions.

BPD Support Groups:

- **The National BPD Organization:** https://www.borderlin epersonalitydisorder.org/ – Offers online support groups and resources specifically for individuals with BPD.
- **The American Psychological Association (APA):** https://w ww.apa.org/ – Provides a searchable database of support groups for various mental health conditions, including BPD.
- **Local Mental Health Clinics or Hospitals:** Many clinics and hospitals offer BPD support groups facilitated by mental health professionals.

Online Resources:

- **The Jed Foundation:** https://jedfoundation.org/ – Provides mental health resources and support for teens and young adults.
- **The Trevor Project:** https://www.thetrevorproject.org/ – Offers crisis intervention and suicide prevention services specifically for LGBTQ+ youth.
- **Crisis Text Line:** Text HOME to 741741 to connect with a crisis counselor via text message.

Hotlines:

- **National Suicide Prevention Lifeline:** 988 – Offers 24/7, accessible, and confidential support for people in distress, as well as prevention and crisis resources for you or your loved ones.
- **Crisis Text Line:** Text HOME to 741741 to connect with a

crisis counselor via text message.
- **The Trevor Project:** 1-866-488-7386 - Provides crisis intervention and suicide prevention services specifically for LGBTQ+ youth.

Life might feel like its an unrelenting crisis or emergency at times.

If you have a diagnosis of borderline personality disorder and are feeling suicidal, self-injurious, or self-destructive, the good news is that there are people who are willing to help.

Whatever you are doing right now, stop and commit to keeping yourself safe and alive for the next hour.

I'm serious. Set the timer on your phone for 60 minutes. Promise yourself that you won't make any problems worse during that time. The truth is that even intense emotions and urges can change within an hour or two. You don't have to add to your pain or trauma. You don't have to hurt others.

Letting people know that you need help is always a smart decision. Keep telling others until they listen.

Suicide Prevention Lifeline

988

Warm Lines

These are peer-run organizations and may not be available 24/7.

Crisis Text Line

If you can't talk, text.

Samaritans NYC

1-212-673-3000

Veterans Crisis Line
1-800-273-8255 (Press 1) or text 838255
RAINN
Sexual assault hotline
1-800-656-4673
National Alliance on Mental Illness (NAMI) Crisis Text Line
Text 741741
Again, if you can't talk, text.

23

Conclusion

"Mental health problems don't define who you are. They are something you experience. You walk in the rain, and you feel the rain, but, importantly, YOU ARE NOT THE RAIN." — Matt Haig.

In conclusion, Borderline Personality Disorder (BPD) is a complex mental health condition that can significantly impact a person's life, characterized by intense emotions, impulsivity,unstable relationships, a distorted sense of self, and finally, the fear of abandonment. However, with the appropriate treatment and self-care strategies, individuals with BPD can embark on a journey toward leading fulfilling and meaningful lives.

As we have learned in earlier chapters, the cause of BPD is

believed to have been a result of many traumas or combinations of genetic, environmental, and neurological factors. Even childhood abuse or neglect can contribute to the cause of BPD.

Treatments typically involve a combination of therapy and medication. Dialectical Behavior Therapy (DBT) is an effective form of therapy for BPD. It teaches individuals skills to manage emotions, improve relationships, and develop healthy coping mechanisms. Other forms of therapy, such as cognitive behavioral therapy (CBT) and schema therapy, may also be beneficial.

Symptomatic medications can be used to manage specific symptoms of BPD, such as depression, anxiety, or impulsivity. However, note that medication alone is not considered a primary treatment for BPD.

In addition to professional treatment, **SELF-CARE** plays a crucial role in managing BPD symptoms and achieving a sense of normalcy. Therefore, the process will include practicing mindfulness, developing healthy coping skills, setting boundaries, building a solid support network, avoiding substance abuse, and practicing self-compassion. These are amply discussed and explained in previous chapters.

Living with BPD is a journey, and it may involve ups and downs. It is essential to keep in mind that recovery is possible, and with the proper support and treatment, individuals with BPD can lead fulfilling and meaningful lives. Hence, two prong system of seeking help from mental health professionals and engaging in self-care strategies are essential steps toward achieving a sense of normalcy and well-being.

Do not forget that every person has some personality disorder, so try to identify which one is within you and immediately work to change yourself to lead a better life.

24

Inspire Someone Else!

Inspire Someone Else!

You have the tools you need, and now it's time to put them to the test...

But before you do, why not take a moment to show someone else the path?

By sharing your honest opinion of this book, reviewing my book on Amazon, and sharing a little about your emotional intelligence journey, you'll help new readers take their first steps on this transformative quest.

Thank you so much for your support!

I'm excited about the journey ahead of you.

Maya A

BBSS Publishing.

BBSS Publishing.

25

Resources

Resources;

Johns Hopkins Medicine. (n.d.). Borderline personality disorder. Johns Hopkins Medicine
   https://www.hopkinsmedicine.org/health/conditions-and-diseases/borderline-personality-disorder

National Alliance on Mental Illness (NAMI). (n.d.). Borderline personality disorder. National Alliance on Mental Illness
   https://www.nami.org/About-Mental-Illness/Mental-Health-Conditions/Borderline-Personality-Disorder

National Institutes of Health. (n.d.). Borderline personality disorder. [Book chapter]. National Institutes of Health (.gov). Retrieved from www.ncbi.nlm.nih.gov/books/NBK430883/

Healthy Pilipinas. (n.d.). Borderline Personality Disorder [SNIPPET]. Healthy Pilipinas. Retrieved from www.healthypilipinas.ph/health-a-z/borderline-personality-disorder

Mayo Clinic. (n.d.). Borderline personality disorder. Mayo Clinic:

https://www.mayoclinic.org/diseases-conditions/borderline -personality-disorder/diagnosis-treatment/drc-20370242

MAYO CLINIC INFORMATION

mayoclinic.com/health/borderline-personality-disorder/ DS00442

Other sites ;

1. slidetodoc.com/emotion-dysregulation-ma
2. https://dictionary.apa.org/borderline-personality-disor der
3. Retrieved from https://castbox.fm/episode/The-Struggl e%3A-Borderline-Personality-Disorder-Pt5-id3388781 -id609015175
4. https://castbox.fm/episode/The-Struggle%3A-Borderlin e-Personality-Disorder-Pt5-id3388781-id609015175
5. **https://www.ncbi.nlm.nih.gov/pmc/articles/PMC2**
6. **https://www.ncbi.nlm.nih.gov/pmc/articles/PMC**
7. DOI:10.9734/bpi/rudhr/v5/8029E;In book: Recent Updates in Disease and Health Research (pp.Page 98-118) , Publisher: B P International
8. www.fsd79.org/Page/2433

About the Author

About the Author

Maya A. has a huge passion for understanding the human mind and society. Maya A., with a graduate degree in Psychology and Sociology, has insatiable curiosity and dedication to unraveling the complexities of the human experience, and this instinct has led him to become a promising in the field of nonfiction publishing, which will help humanity.

When not immersed in the world of words, Maya A. is busy keeping himself fit. He is a keen sportsman and fitness freak. He believes a healthy body is the foundation for a healthy mind and practices what he preaches. Whether it's hitting the gym, running marathons, or exploring new outdoor adventures, Maya embraces the exhilaration of physical activity to find balance and clarity in his own life.

With Maya A. as your guide, you can be assured of a transformative journey through the pages of his books. Prepare to be enlightened, challenged, and inspired as you deeply explore the human experience.

Also by Maya A

Dubai Travel Guide for Beginners

Other Books by Maya A
Dubai Travel Guide For Beginners is one of the world's most popular tourist destinations and vacation spots. This book condenses everything to help you plan a successful trip to Dubai into a pocket-sized guide.

2.**Multi Notebook With Plain and Lined Pages**

https://www.amazon.com/dp/B0CJXDSMB7

3. **Alphabet Handwriting Practice Book**

By BBS Self Publishing

https://www.amazon.com/dp/B0CTQHX3DY

4.**Thanksgiving day Guest book with dinner party planner**

https://www.amazon.com/dp/B0CN1HZJ5V

5.**Mike's PAT Testing Logbook** for recording PAT inspection and safety Inspection data, a Unique combo for recording data both company-wise and appliance-wise.

https://www.amazon.com/dp/B0CNWNZ9NF

6. **Alphabet Learning and Writing for preschool, Nursery, K+3 kids, learning ABC with visual aids, Learn writing by tracing for capital and small fond and A to Z on practice sheets**

https://www.amazon.com/dp/B0CPC1VQCZ

7. Coming soon: **Exploring The Secrets Of Enigmatic Lakshadweep.**

By Maya A